God's Tent Pitched Among Us

A New Pattern for Rural Church Mission

— BENJAMIN CARTER —

Sacristy
Press

Sacristy Press
PO Box 612, Durham, DH1 9HT

www.sacristy.co.uk

First published in 2020 by Sacristy Press, Durham

Sacristy Limited, registered in England & Wales, number 7565667

British Library Cataloguing-in-Publication Data
A catalogue record for the book is available from the British Library

ISBN 978-1-78959-097-5

Foreword

My go-to translation of the *New Testament* is that of a former colleague of mine, Fr Nick King SJ. His translation of the Johannine prologue includes the following: "And the Word became flesh and pitched his tent among us." There is no better understanding of the Word, Jesus Christ: he is on the move, and we should expect to be surprised by the results. Imagine then, as Benjamin recounts in his introduction, you are "out and about" Tynedale and you happen to see "a six-metre bell tent pitched in a field". One week you might see it by a river, and another week you might spy it on a hilltop. You might be curious, intrigued even. This book is the story of that tent, but it looks beyond the canvas and encourages us through its lived wisdom to set about pitching God's tent in our own context. The book was written in part as a response to the author's own wrestling with identity and nationhood amidst the upheaval of the political landscape in recent years, something to which I also relate (born in Scotland, grew up in the north-east of England). What Benjamin could not have known (as indeed none of us could) was the profound global impact of the COVID-19 virus which has left us all #doingchurchdifferently. This book speaks into that context now, and what a gift it is in that respect when I for one have had to attend to being a little more creative than usual in how I convey the message of God's love in Jesus Christ. All of us, regardless of churchmanship (or even if church and organized religion features very minimally in our lives) ought to be challenged by the realization that our church buildings are a gift, but they are not who we are. I learnt this in a very real way whilst serving as a bishop in Aotearoa New Zealand, where following the Canterbury earthquakes of 2011 many church buildings were either destroyed or closed due to lack of earthquake strengthening. We don't all face natural disasters of course; however, as the *Mission-shaped Church* report quoted in this book tells us, we better start thinking creatively outwards rather than solely maintaining the "inner" lives of our church buildings. Again, they (alone) are not who we are.

One of the great learning points of the COVID-19 crisis is the rapid professional development involved in taking services online. By and large, communities have embraced this positively. It has demonstrated that you don't need to be an expert to be creative, nor do you need to read a complex manual or go on a 6-week course. What we must not lose sight of is depth and understanding, and that is where this book comes in very handy. The author's admission that no one involved in the God's Tent project were experts in Fresh Expressions is refreshing. What was and is important is the attitude of being open to God's Spirit, and here our story reconnects in a very real way with the emergence of the life of the Early Church. As the project developed, it sought to listen to the environment, tradition, and people of differing ages and experiences. The Tent is not apart from its contextual history and social dynamic, it is richly a part of it. This model of engagement is fully transferable to diverse settings and even offers a way of re-engaging with locale. As I stand in my village where we live, I can ask questions of story, narrative, identity and history. What if I pitched God's Tent "here", what might that look like? It's also a challenge to look at our church buildings afresh, as carriers of the gospel, heralds of the kingdom. Buildings may not be who we are, but they can remind of who we were or who we can be.

Part 2 builds on the solid theological and pastoral foundations of what goes before. It might seem odd to use words like "solid" and "foundations", but the challenge here is to view these words fluidly. The Church after all, has always adapted to place, only we might have forgotten what that feels like at times. The practical nature of the reflections and liturgies offered in this part of the book evoke the somewhat practical atmosphere that pitching any tent provides. Wellies on outside, wellies off inside. This is sacred space, and we are a pilgrim people who gather found the "fire" to listen, proclaim, and be sent out to wonder anew at the world we live, love and learn in. Where can I "pitch God's tent" today?

The Rt Revd Dr Helen-Ann Hartley
Bishop of Ripon

Acknowledgements

This book is the product of one of the most fruitful and enjoyable periods of my ordained ministry. As such it owes as much to the people and communities in the Benefice of Haydon Bridge and Beltingham with Henshaw (Parishes by the Wall), to which I am fortunate to minister, as it does to me. So my first thanks go to the Churchwardens, Parochial Church Councils and wider church communities of these parishes, not least for the generosity of the Mission Funds of both these parishes, and of Hexham Deanery in the Diocese of Newcastle, for funding the purchase of our tent and linked equipment. As I say again and again in this book, God's Tent is defined by the community that has been formed in and through it. I have been very grateful to colleagues who have helped me in the leadership of God's Tent, and who have been constant conversation partners on the way as I have tried to collect these experiences and thoughts into this book. When I speak of the "we" of God's Tent I am speaking of the invaluable support I have received from Gill Alexander, Tim Burdon, James Feeley, Chloe Lowdon, Phil Simm and Jeremy Thompson. Alongside these leaders, God's Tent has been blessed to host and be hosted by many who, like me, are fortunate to live in the beauty of the South Tyne Valley. These include friends in the Parishes by the Wall, as well as in the Parishes of St John Lee, Warden and Newbrough, and Haltwhistle and Greenhead who are too many for me to mention here without forgetting some. I would, though, like to acknowledge the assistance of Caroline Cope, Mandy Roberts, and Gillian Teasdale of Northumberland National Park and The Sill National Landscape Discovery Centre, who were generous enough to lend us a tent and a space for our first ever pitching and have remained generous and willing friends to God's Tent ever since.

Much of the content of the first part of this book has grown from conversations I have had with Jeremy Auld, Tom Birch, Bishop Nicholas

Chamberlain, Peter Dobson, Dyfrig Ellis, Ruth Elmes, Nigel Hardaker, Stuart Jones, Sophie Langman, Anna Maloney, Bishop Mark Tanner and Judith Sadler. In addition, Alan Bartlett, Michael Sadgrove and Rachel Wood read and commented generously on earlier drafts of this book. My parents, Richard and Awena Carter, have supported me in the completion of this book. My wife, Steph Carter, and as our children Elizabeth and Matilda, have supported and encouraged me more than I can say through the inception of this project and production of this book. Steph has also proofread the whole text and allowed me to correct countless errors; leaving me responsible for the ones which remain.

It is to Steph that this book is dedicated with love, for pitching her tent with me.

Contents

Introduction

At 3 p.m. on the third Sunday of the month, if you are out and about in Tynedale in west Northumberland, you might see a six-metre bell tent pitched in a field, by a river or on a hilltop. This is God's Tent. Gathered there you will find a mixed group of children, parents and young adults exploring stories of faith and God's love for us in the landscape of Northumberland. This book tells the story of God's Tent.

On one level this book exists as an introduction and guide to how to begin to pitch God's Tent in different contexts. So, in this book, particularly in Part Two, you will find practical advice for what you might need to do and to be to pitch God's Tent. Along with this you will find a series of sample "pitchings"—as we describe our gatherings or worship in God's Tent. These are some of the ways in which we have explored our faith, through the richness of the Christian tradition, in the glory of our creation. All of these have worked. They also act as a blueprint or guide through which you might develop your own pitchings of God's Tent. We pitch in a river valley, so we find rivers and trees as well as moorland and meadows to explore. This affects the stories we tell and the pitchings we follow. A different landscape will offer itself to different stories and experiences and so these sample pitchings offer not just some "recipes" for you to follow, but the shape and pattern for pitching God's Tent.

God's Tent did not, however, spring up in a vacuum. It is the result of the pressures, challenges and opportunities that we have found in our parishes. As a consequence, this book is a recognition of this context. So, this book also exists as a reflection on the contemporary debates and conversations in the Church of England over the future mission and ministry of the Church. Beginning with the *Mission-shaped Church* report, and then coloured by the *Renewal and Reform* programme of recent years, the Church of England is going through a period of change which has not been seen in generations. God's Tent has been born in the midst of these debates and so acts, in a small way, as a worked example of how we might begin to navigate what I call in chapter 1 the frontier between the inheritance of the Church and its call to innovation. Part 1 of this book therefore acts as a reflection on the contemporary status and challenges of this debate in the Church and how, through God's Tent, we have tried to engage productively with it.

This book can therefore be read in two parts—as guidebook and as reflection. But I hope that you will read it as a whole. It is a worked understanding of the deep creative richness of the metaphor of our God who "pitches his tent among us". In chapter 3, I reflect a little more deeply on the richness of this great scriptural picture of a tent-pitching God, which we find first in the book of Exodus, then echoing through the Old Testament. Most powerfully for us we find this rich theological picture in the prologue to John's Gospel.

In focusing so singularly on this one biblical picture, and reflecting through this book on this central biblical story, there is a danger that this could all seem a little naive at best, and at worst the kind of ecclesial gimmick which the defenders of inherited models of church are so anxious about; as if the process of the development of God's Tent, and the writing of this book for that matter, have been a process of searching biblical concordances for the use of the word "Tent" as a justification for both our monthly activities and the rationale of this book. I believe and hope that my approach has been more profound and subtle than that. God's Tent is an attempt to live in, through and with the stories of God's love for all creation. Our starting point for this is not creation itself, but the stories we have lived and consumed through the pages of scripture. Biblical scholars like Walter Brueggemann have taught us that these texts are not simply historical records but the "imaginative remembering" of the great story of God's love by communities formed in and through that ongoing story.[1] As we will see in chapters 2 and 3, the pattern of our mission and the story of a "tent-pitching" God become powerful stories through which we can make sense of our experience and story. God's Tent in its form and structure seeks to live in and through this story. We do this both explicitly through the pitching of a tent and imaginatively in the way we use the story and narrative of scripture and tradition to inform our worship and experience of God in creation. God's Tent is, to borrow N. T. Wright's famous illustration, an attempt to play out the final act of the "five-act play" as a deliberate and faithful improvisation on the recurring biblical theme of the tent-pitching God.[2]

The God who pitches his tent among us is not only a defining picture for how we can understand who God is through the imaginative remembering of the Old Testament. As we shall see, this picture was developed by the first Christians to understand who God is for us in Jesus. Through reflecting and improvising on this picture of a tent-pitching God we are, in God's Tent, finding a creative way to explore this story of who God is, and in it become a worshipping community formed and created in relationship to our tent-pitching God.

Part 1

Living Faith on the Frontier

In his 2016 book *The Marches* the writer and politician Rory Stewart reflects on the deep and pervasive power that borders and frontiers play in our culture and society. Written within the backdrop of the Scottish Independence Referendum of 2014, Stewart, through an account of his walk along Hadrian's Wall and then from his home in Cumbria to his childhood home in Scotland, reflects on the deep power that frontiers have to define who we think we are, and how we respond to the world around us. As the MP for an English constituency, his job would remain whatever the result of the impending vote. But, as the son of a Scottish father and an English mother, Stewart found that "[j]ust over 4 million of the 61 million people in the United Kingdom were told they could decide whether the island of Britain should be split in two". If the result of the referendum had gone the other way, "I would still have a constituency," Stewart writes, but as a Unionist, "I would no longer have a country."[3]

I am, like Rory Stewart, the product of a British family. Born and brought up in England, my father is English and my mother is Welsh. Although I have not walked the Anglo-Welsh borders of my identity as thoroughly as Stewart has his, a childhood travelling literally and metaphorically along the Welsh Marches has left a deep impression on me. For this reason, I shared with Rory Stewart the same anxieties as the Scottish Referendum approached that something of my "British" identity would be lost because of the political decisions over the contested nature of this frontier. All this reminds us that frontiers matter. At the time of writing the United Kingdom remains paralysed in its attempts to remake and understand its frontier with the European Union. In the United States of America, President Trump has traded on the political capital of his southern border. In both these cases, these borders, these frontiers, act as a dividing line. Whether they are accidents of geography, lines of political or military expediency or deep lines of cultural difference, frontiers carry with them a value and power and creativity to divide or unite us.

The work of this book is something of the product of the creativity that comes from living on a frontier. The parishes I serve take in the central section of Hadrian's Wall; we describe ourselves as the "Parishes by the Wall". Although, as Rory Stewart would remind us, this ancient line was an artificial border, it has always created meaning. It was at the time of construction a sign of military power. But it was also a symbol of political failure: though the Romans always saw Britain as one island, the wall was a recognition that they could not master the island of the Britons totally, as they had mastered many of the other indigenous peoples of Europe and the Mediterranean. As we know more about this ancient frontier, we discover that it was a cultural dividing line as well as a point of economic convergence. Even in the centuries after the Romans left, this frontier remained. Not always a political line, it became a place of military control, of artistic creativity, a location of learning and exploration, and now a place of heritage, of exercise and, for some, spiritual encounter. This is not a book on Hadrian's Wall, but it is a book which has been born in and through the creative tensions and opportunities which come from living in the shadow of this ancient frontier.

In the Parishes by the Wall we have embraced this reality by describing ourselves as "Living Faith on the Frontier". In this simple statement we have tried to describe who and what we are seeking to be as a church. God's Tent has grown as one of the fruits of this aspiration. As we explore God's Tent, it is worth spending some time reflecting on one of the deepest "frontiers" within the life of the contemporary Church, the frontier between "inheritance" and "innovation". The Church of England is currently facing a period of great challenge. Culturally, it no longer serves a nation which is uniformly Christian in identity. Regular Sunday attendance in church has been falling for decades. Financial and human resources are increasingly put under pressure. In the face of this potentially existential crisis a debate has developed in the Church which runs along the frontier between inheritance and innovation. On one side of this frontier is the belief that the Church needs to protect and maintain its inheritance of parishes and churches. The most passionate defenders of this side of the frontier, like the theologian John Milbank, see any movement to undermine this historical inheritance not simply as a strategic error but as "a clear conspiracy against the parish" and a "blasphemous denial" of the true nature and calling of the Church.[4] On the other side of this frontier we find theologians like Pete Ward who advocate for the root and branch innovation of the Church. We need, Ward argues, "a new reformation to renew and refresh our church if it is to be faithful to its purpose and its Lord".[5]

Both these positions are extreme examples of the positions taken between inheritance and innovation, but they are also not unique positions in the experience of the Church of England. Faced by the enormous cultural changes of the twentieth century theologians and missiologists have again and again sought to understand the challenges of living on this frontier. Writing from a Roman Catholic perspective, Stephen Bevans and Roger Schroeder have recognized this frontier in these terms:

> Christian mission is both anchored in fidelity to the past and challenged to fidelity in the present. It must preserve, defend and proclaim the *constants* of the church's traditions; at the same time it must respond creatively and boldly to the *contexts* in which it finds itself.[6]

Writing from the other end of the theological spectrum, Christopher Wright also recognizes the challenge of living on this frontier between inheritance and innovation. Responding in particular to the cultural pluralism which defines much of the (post)modern experience of the West, he argues that Christian mission has always lived on this frontier:

> Cultural plurality is nothing new for Christian mission. It is rather the very stuff of missional engagement and missiological reflection. We may be challenged by swimming in the postmodern pool, but we need not feel out of our depth here.[7]

God's Tent was conceived and first experienced in the context of a Church of England parish, and so the frontiers which define this experience are those that run through the life of the contemporary Church of England. However, as we have seen, the challenge of living on the frontier between inheritance and innovation is one which infuses all Christian traditions. Like all frontiers this division in the life of the contemporary Church can operate in two ways. It can either be a deep impermeable border, defining "us" from "them", or it can be a place and space of intellectual and theological creativity. God's Tent, pitching itself firmly and confidently across this frontier, offers a different way of navigation between the two, where a deeper sense of who God is calling us to be comes only when we recognize ourselves as living our faith on the frontier. In this way, God's Tent provides a response which could be used in different contexts and traditions. It is, though, one which comes, initially, with an Anglican accent.

Mission-shaped Church

This is not the first book to recognize that the Church of England is living through challenging times. Fewer and fewer people worship in our churches Sunday by Sunday. This decline is mirrored in the statistics that show that church is no longer the default location for the celebrations and commemorations of family life in the occasional offices of christenings, weddings and funerals. Both these markers of decline relate to a third area of concern, that the Church has less money than it used to have. The financial pressures on the Church (which are linked to these two former factors) mean that there is a growing realization that the Church of England's vision of itself as "a Christian presence in every community" is not one which can be taken for granted. This challenge is not a new one. By most markers, Sunday attendance in church has halved in nearly half a century. Alongside that, Christian identity has declined steadily over this same period. Some of this can be explained by the increasingly multicultural make-up of the population of the UK. However, alongside this change there has been a growth in those who actively assert that they have either no religion, no faith or identify as "spiritual" but not "religious".[8]

Within the life of the Church of England the reality of these changes was first truly accepted in the publication of the *Mission-shaped Church* report in 2004. The report sets itself from the outset against the inherited missional life of the Church. The authors of the report noted that the inherited missional strategy of the Church was a "returners" strategy, waiting for those who had drifted away from church in their youth to return as they got older. However, as the report points out, this strategy contained within it a law of diminishing returns. As the religious identity of Britain changed there were fewer and fewer returners to attract back to church. Britain has become, in the words of the report, a country made up of shrinking groups of regular attenders, and growing populations of the de-churched—those who have had some contact with church in the past—and the non-churched—who have never had any meaningful connection to church or the Christian faith.

In the face of this dilemma the *Mission-shaped Church* report recommended a fundamental realignment of the Church of England towards patterns of innovation in mission. However, it was not simply this realignment of priorities around mission which made the report so controversial. The deepest and abiding assertion of *Mission-shaped Church* was its advocacy that money and resources were urgently needed to support innovation over inheritance in the Church of England. In particular, *Mission-shaped Church* argued that if the Church was to reach out to the de-churched and non-churched populations within our society it needed to respond to them as the wider population responded to the world around it, as consumers. In perhaps the most contentious claim of the report the authors argued:

> We have moved from a society that shaped its members primarily
> as producers—those who believed in progress and in producing
> something that contributed to the better life that was certain to
> come through education and hard work—to a society that shapes
> its members first and foremost by the need to play the role of
> consumer . . . The core value of society has moved from 'progress'
> to 'choice'—the absolute right of freedom to choose.[9]

By accepting that modern Britain is now defined by choice above all things, *Mission-shaped Church* asked how does the Church respond to this culture of choice? At the heart of this was a movement away from the inherited missional strategy of the Church of England, which is to remain and wait for people to "come to us". Instead the authors suggest that there is now an opportunity to change this emphasis, and for the Church to "go to them".

The passionate call of *Mission-shaped Church* set up a strategy for how the Church should navigate the frontier from inheritance into innovation. Moving across this frontier *Mission-shaped Church* argued that the Church needed to call "Pioneers", a new brand of ordained ministry trained and sent out to work across this new frontier, to discern, innovate and form new expressions of church life. Drawing inspiration from the Declaration of Assent—where all ordained ministers in the Church of England assent to proclaim the gospel "afresh in each generation"—these pioneers would create "Fresh Expressions of Church", new ways of being and experiencing church. Some of these would be grafted onto traditional patterns of church life, like Messy Church or Café Church, seeking to reach the de-churched on the fringe of traditional church life. Others would seek to engage with the networks of modern life—through work, sports clubs, shared interests—meeting the de-churched and non-churched where they were to create and grow the church in places and spaces which the inherited models of the Church were unable to reach.

The *Mission-shaped Church* report, and the initiatives that grew from it, inevitably created waves within the life of the Church of England, with opposition running along the frontier between inheritance and innovation. This is seen no more clearly than in Andrew Davison and Alison Milbank's 2010 book *For the Parish: A Critique of Fresh Expressions*. Central to this book is a critique of the use of consumerism and personal choice in the life of the Church of England. "It is notable," Davison and Milbank argue, "that every Fresh Expression starts with what is *chosen*, whereas the inherited church is more likely to start with what is *given*."[10] The failure of *Mission-shaped Church*, for Davison and Milbank, has not been in their analysis of the world; rather its over-eagerness to prioritize innovation over the inherited gifts and strengths of the Church. It is not the case, Davison and Milbank argue, that a world which thirsts for more choice is best served by more choice. Rather, they argue, the more fluid and changeable the world becomes, the greater the necessity, virtue and immutability of what the Church has always offered becomes. For them this is already present in the ancient organization of the parish.[11]

The path of *Mission-shaped Church* away from the inherited models of church is one which, Milbank and Davison argue, cannot be overstated. The parish is a universal model because its geography ensures that "no one is excluded".[12] By contrast, *Mission-shaped Church*, Fresh Expressions and the related focus on the growth of church-going congregations turns the Church away from its call to act as the chaplains to the nation. "*Mission-shaped Church* is a turning point in the self-understanding of the Church of England," Davison and Milbank argue. "With it, our doctrine of the Church has leapt, not drifted, in the direction of Free Church Protestantism."[13]

Renewal and Reform

If *Mission-shaped Church* challenged the Church of England to reform its missional life from inheritance to innovation, then a positive option for innovation was made by the Church of England through the inauguration of the *Renewal and Reform* programme in 2015. In *Renewal and Reform* the Church of England has set itself, what itself describes as, "an ambitious programme of work, which seeks to provide a narrative of hope to the Church of England in the 21st century".[14] The backdrop of *Renewal and Reform*, as with *Mission-shaped Church*, was a recognition of both the steady decline in regular Sunday attendance, the ageing profile of the clergy of the Church of England and the increased financial challenge of maintaining parish ministry across the country. The radical move at the heart of the *Renewal and Reform* programme was to bring the impetus for mission and innovation, which *Mission-shaped Church* had advocated, into the mainstream of the Church. In particular, this was achieved by a prioritization of the Church's financial resources towards programmes for innovation over inheritance.

Until the advent of *Renewal and Reform* diocesan finances were founded on the money raised from regular giving and supplemented fees and the historic assets of each diocese. For dioceses serving historically poorer parts of England, a "central allocation" was made to subsidise the ministry of the Church of England in those places that could not traditionally afford the cost of ministry. Within the *Renewal and Reform* programme this money from central funds was now split into two different funds. One, the *Lowest Income Community Funding*, uses information on population, income and deprivation levels to target support to the most deprived communities in England. The second, *Strategic Development Funding*, is available for dioceses to bid for innovative projects focused on missional and spiritual growth. Although the traditional patterns of diocesan funding remain in place—giving, fees and investments—in *Renewal and Reform* the central church has made a clear choice to direct its funds towards innovation over inheritance. As the archbishops stated in 2015, "[i]n short, such funds will have a bias to the poor and a commitment to spiritual and numerical growth".[15] The *Renewal and Reform* programme provides for the most radical and deep-rooted reorganization of the Church of England resources and practices for over a century. Writing from the context of the rural church it also carries with it a series of challenges and unintended consequences.

It is fair to say that the Church of England is disproportionately rural. Government figures calculate that about 9.3 million, or 17.6 per cent of the population in England, live in rural locations. However, against this two-thirds of the parishes of the Church of England and 65 per cent of church buildings are in rural areas. Alongside this distribution of parishes and buildings, 40 per cent of the worshipping population of the Church of England is in rural churches. This proportion rises at festivals, with almost half of those attending church at Christmas doing so in rural churches. Historically, the numerical weighting of the Church towards rural contexts has been mirrored in the distribution of resources. Although this is not a perfect marker, we can see this through the distribution of clergy numbers across the Church of England: 43 per cent of incumbents, 40 per cent of curates and 47 per cent of self-supporting ministers work in rural locations. If the distribution of all clergy is taken as a mark of resource then in urban England there is one member of the clergy per 7,330 head of population, whereas in rural England the number drops to 2,116. However, when human resource is placed against the historical inheritance of the Church—parishes and church buildings—the picture changes. In urban contexts, there are 1.3 clergy for every building and 1.7 clergy for every parish, whereas in rural locations there are 0.2 clergy for every building and 0.25 clergy for every parish.[16]

It must be noted that clergy numbers are not the only mark of resource and strength within the life of the Church. However, using them as a base, however crude, throws into stark relief the challenge faced by the rural church. Returning to the frontier between inheritance and innovation, it is possible to argue that the disproportionate weighting of the Church's inheritance and attendance to the rural church shows that this is where the inheritance runs deepest. However, such is the scale of this inheritance, in parishes and buildings, that this comes at a great cost in terms of finance and human resource. So, the rural church has experienced generations of ongoing reform with the increased grouping of parishes into multi-parish benefices under the leadership of increasingly stretched clergy; all at the same time seeking to maintain the buildings, structures and worship which are part of the warp and weft of the inherited life of the Church. However, as the Church of England, through the *Renewal and Reform* programme, has prioritized resources toward areas of innovation there has necessarily been a cost felt in the rural church which carries, disproportionately, the weight of the inherited life of the Church. Through focusing of resources with a "bias" towards the poor and growth, *Renewal and Reform* has seen a removal of many of the financial supports which implicitly underpinned much of the inheritance of the Church. The often-unseen cost of this has been the effect this has had on the rural church. With a focus on "average" income, rather than "median" income or deprivation of service, *Lower Income Community Funding* unintentionally prioritizes the needs of poor communities in urban contexts, which can be adequately judged by the mark of average income, against the very real, but very often hidden, needs of rural poverty, which are only truly revealed when median income or deprivation of service is taken into account.[17] Similarly, the focus of projects supported by *Strategic Development Funding* on numerical growth naturally shows a bias to projects focused in higher population areas, such as the establishment of city-centre "Resource" churches. Of the nearly £116 million allocated by the *Strategic Development Fund* just under 19 per cent (£19.7 million) has been for projects which include a rural aspect. Very often these projects begin with an urban focus with the intention that this work will radiate out into rural contexts. Of the total allocated only just under 2 per cent (£2.27 million) has been allocated for projects with a uniquely rural focus.[18] Advocates for *Renewal and Reform* would argue that in straitened times the Church needs to use its precious resources more carefully and judiciously. Critics have seen this reordering of the Church's resources away from the inherited church, and through that from the traditional strengths of the rural church, as a sign of the inevitable movement of the Church across the frontier from inheritance to innovation.

Living faith on the frontier

Life on a frontier can go one of two ways. The first is that the frontier, however real or tangible, creates an opposition, a sense of "them" and "us". The second is that life on a frontier encourages a creative engagement with what lies on the other side. Within the Church of England, as we have lived through debates between the virtues of inheritance and innovation, it is not hard to find, as we have already seen, responses of opposition. Writing in 2006, in the initial debates following the publication of *Mission-shaped Church*, Rowan Williams—then Archbishop of Canterbury—acknowledged this problem. "People," Williams lamented, "throw around the word 'sectarian' with some abandon in debates".[19] This reality, Williams writes, is not just a sign of lament, but a sign of intellectual failure. Drawing on a theme deep within his own theological work, Williams argues that the challenge of Christian life is not to pick a side, but to live with the complexity that comes from being open to the fullness of the debate we are living through. This is none other than the call to live with orthodoxy. As Williams argues:

> The idea of 'orthodoxy', which some find so frightening, is really about the struggle to keep our language transparent to the truth of Jesus, resisting ways of speaking and understanding that reduce or domesticate this radical truth.[20]

The challenge of Christian faith comes, Williams argues, from recognizing that we are living at all times on a frontier. A frontier between the human and the divine, between the Church and the world, between the call to serve the signs of kingdom around us and to strive for the kingdom that is yet to come. Christian theology, Williams argues, has always been a struggle to keep this debate open. As he argues elsewhere:

> Orthodoxy's challenge to the individual or to the local and specific group need not be seen as a threat to some sort of absolute spiritual independence: it is rather a challenge to the shrinking of a tradition to the dimension of one person's or one group's need for comfort or control.[21]

Within the context of the debates that developed in the wake of *Mission-shaped Church*, the challenge for the Church is not to pitch too firmly on one side of the frontier or another. The challenge is to live and flourish in the "both/and" which lies at the heart of Christian faith.

Simon Oliver makes a similar argument in his reflection on the numerical growth experienced in cathedrals over recent years. This, he argues, has come through the implicit ability of cathedrals to hold together different integrities. The implicit virtue of a cathedral, he argues, is that it can be a unifying middle space between the individual and the otherness of the world around us. This middle path, Oliver argues, follows the *via media* which lies at the heart of Anglican identity. This is not simply the balanced middle-way between the doctrinal poles of Protestantism and Catholicism which marked the territory of the Reformation. Instead, Oliver draws on the theology of Lancelot Andrewes to articulate the deep value of the *via media* or "middle trajectory" between God and man, and earth and heaven. "In other words the *via media* is as much about heaven meeting earth as it is about doctrinal moderation," Oliver argues:

> And where does heaven meet earth salvifically, other than in the Word incarnate? So the Church is a *via media* in the sense that it shares in the life of Christ at the joining of heaven and earth and the gathering into unity of divine and human natures. [22]

For Oliver the recent flourishing of cathedrals has come in their ability to use their architecture, history and material treasures to create a tangible spiritual otherness which has the power to "penetrate the modern sense of spiritual alienation, self-determination, and autonomy".[23] Mirroring Williams' argument, Oliver shows the missional power that comes when we do not simply respond and innovate in response to the apparent needs of the world around us, but hold these needs in relation to the inherited virtues of riches of the Church.

Williams' call for an openness of language and Oliver's recasting of the Anglican *via media* draw us back to the wisdom we find in Rory Stewart's *The Marches*, that when we remain open to what lies on both sides of the frontier, we are able to find ourselves more truly. Writing from the perspective of the rural church it would be tempting to rest in the values of our inheritance and look jealously at the resources being directed to the innovation on the other side of this frontier. Similarly, for those motivated to innovate in all things, the rural church and its challenges can seem a foreign country far removed from the excitement and possibilities of urban church growth. However, if we have the courage to live on this frontier and allow our faith to grow there, we find the deep resources that are available to us as we draw from our inheritance, harnessing the spirit of innovation which calls us to proclaim the good news of Jesus Christ afresh in each generation. God's Tent is a living example of what this can look like. It is not a perfect one and neither is it the only one. However, it offers a pattern and structure for missional innovation within the context of the inherited church which comes from embracing the life of faith lived on the frontier.

CHAPTER 2

Mission on the Move

God's Tent did not begin life in a vacuum. Like all missional endeavours it began life as a response to a perceived need. This chapter will tell the story of how we moved from responding in prayer to this need to a continually-developing expression of church. I begin with this story for two reasons. The first is that it helps set the scene for what comes after, why we made the choices we did and how it has changed and developed over quite a short period of time from "something for the older children" to an expression of church in its own right. The second reason is that we hope this will act as an inspiration to others. Prior to the establishment of God's Tent, none of us who were involved would call ourselves experts on mission, or on the outdoors, or in Fresh Expressions. However, like many in the Church, we found ourselves living on the frontier of inheritance and innovation, and our experience of this developed into God's Tent. There is, therefore, a truth in saying that if we can create something which has flourished like God's Tent, then others can too. That might be by following our example, as later chapters and particularly the second part of this book will encourage you to do. It might also be that the journey we have taken acts as inspiration and a map for you to follow, and in doing so to discover where the Spirit is guiding you, as we believe the Spirit has guided us in the conception, development and pitching of God's Tent.

As I have reflected on this journey, the story of Philip's encounter with the Ethiopian eunuch from chapter 8 of the book of Acts (Acts 8:26–end) has provided a powerful lens through which to understand the missional process we have followed. At a very basic level, this story draws us into the deep missional movement of God through history. As Stephen Bevans and Roger Schroeder have commented, in Acts 8: "God is moving the community beyond its borders . . . [as] . . . God was constantly doing in

Israel's history. And the members of the Way were responding."[24] The movement of God's mission, which we are called to join with, is outward. Therefore, our mission must look out beyond the known—our buildings, our patterns of worship, our existing relationships—towards where God is already active and at work in the world. God's Tent does this.

Beyond this deep movement told in the story of Philip and the eunuch, this story provides four moments on which we have found it helpful to reflect, and which provide the pattern for the development and discernment of what we have done. These are: to listen to the Spirit (Acts 8:26); to move quickly (Acts 8:30); to engage with the deep wisdom of tradition (Acts 8:35); and to get out of the way (Acts 8:39).

Listening to the Spirit

Then an angel of the Lord said to Philip, "Get up and go".

Acts 8:26a

God's Tent did not begin with a voice from an angel, or a blinding light or a vision in a dream. But it did begin with a series of prompts and ideas which have felt guided by the Spirit in our midst. The first was a regular question we would ask in our parishes: " . . . and what can we do for older children?" This question recurred again and again in our Messy Church planning sessions (and one which might be familiar to you as well) as we began to think about what we could offer for older children who were beginning to grow out of our Messy Church. This was not a criticism of Messy Church, but a recognition that offering worship for children means that not all age groups can be catered for in the same place at the same time. The reality was that, alongside a thriving Messy Church cohort of early-years children, we were encountering a group of children, and boys in particular, who were moving from the world of crafts and colouring-in to football and Minecraft. What, we would ask again and again, can we offer for these older children?

The second prompt was that the church buildings we had did not offer themselves to new and flexible patterns of worship or activity. Faced with what to do for older children, churches have traditionally looked to establish youth clubs or engage with uniformed organizations. The problem was that we did not have a suitable space where we could follow this tried and trusted path. Our particular inheritance of buildings, although beautiful and much loved, come with the traditional conundrums related to church furnishing and heating which make new activities, let alone creative acts of worship, hard to develop. Perhaps most tellingly in one church, where the vestry is only partially partitioned from the nave, our monthly Sunday School, if the weather allows, gathers on rugs in the churchyard so as not to drown out the sermon and intercessions, or be drowned out themselves by the organ during the hymns.

The final prompt came from the world around us. If the movement of mission is outwards, then we are blessed to be called to move outwards into some of the finest landscapes in Britain. The Parishes by the Wall is possibly the only benefice in the Church of England which includes within its boundaries an Area of Outstanding Natural Beauty (the North Pennines AONB), a National Park (Northumberland National Park) and a World Heritage Site (Hadrian's Wall Frontiers of the Roman Empire UNESCO World Heritage Site). To move out means, by definition, moving into this glorious landscape.

Faced with these three questions one answer presented itself to us almost out of nowhere: buy a large tent. It would be something fun and different for our older children, something cheaper and quicker to erect than a new church building or hall, and something which would take us into the heart of the landscape we wanted to explore. In chapter 3, we will reflect more deeply on the deep theological resonance of the tent "pitched amongst us" in the story of God's mission. But as this idea formed, we found in the tent an idea which drew these three disparate prompts together. This may or may not have been a prompt from an angel but, like Philip, we followed it none the less, and decided to buy a tent, and get up and go.

Moving quickly

> Then the Spirit said to Philip, "Go over to this chariot and join
> it." So Philip ran up to it.
>
> *Acts 8:29–30a*

The part of the story of Philip and the Ethiopian eunuch many remember is the slightly comic image of Philip running to catch up with the chariot as it passed him by. This moment in the story is a reminder that God can often be moving more quickly than we might imagine. In the context of the Church of England, and the rural church in particular, this is a counter-intuitive idea. The perception of rural life is that it moves more slowly, more sedately, and that for many people is its attraction. It is why burnt-out executives "downsize" to the country and why many retire into our villages and small towns. Add to this the Church of England's institutional desire to take time, to consult, to check and double check, and this slower pace is something we can simply assume to be hardwired into the life of the church in rural England. But sometimes God has other ideas. Sometimes the Spirit whispers in our ear, as it did to Philip, "run and join it".

The need to move quickly has been part of the character of God's Tent as it has developed and grown. The first reason for this is that sometimes in small communities we need to move quickly or the opportunity will be lost. As I have already said, one of the initial prompts for God's Tent was to respond to the needs of older children and their families. In rural areas where the relative cohorts of children with whom we engage in church or through schools can fluctuate widely we happened to have contact with a good number of older (key-stage two and older) children. But there was no guarantee that that group would wait for us to catch up with them. In addition, we were finding that many of their parents, who had come to church first through Messy Church, wanted to find out more about faith, but that our inherited model of church was, for the moment, not right for them. Alongside this we also found that we had a smaller group of young adults enquiring about faith both through traditional church and opportunities for discipleship. In these three overlapping groups we had been given a wonderful opportunity. The reality was, however, that we needed to move quickly to respond before the opportunity fizzled out and became something that we might have done had we thought about it. So, we decided to follow Philip's example and move quickly, going from initial thoughts and conversations to our first pitching in about three months.

This imperative to move quickly has remained. Quite soon it became clear to us that God's Tent was much more than simply an afternoon activity for older children, but that it was a fully-fledged expression of church in its own right. So, quickly we had to move our thinking and approach to respond to the adults, as well as children, who were being gathered to God's Tent. We found that they wanted to know more about God and to deepen their faith, and so we moved quickly from our initial conversations to offering and preparing those gathered to God's Tent for baptism and confirmation. God, as Philip found out, wants us to get up and run sometimes, and sometimes we need to move more quickly than we might first imagine to catch up with what God is already doing in our midst.

Engaging with tradition

> Then Philip began to speak, and starting with this scripture, he proclaimed to him the good news about Jesus.
>
> *Acts 8:35*

If we have been encouraged to move quickly in God's Tent this does not mean that we have been hurried or hastened on. Far from it. In moving quickly, we do not ignore what has gone before. Drawing from the ideas explored in the previous chapter, in our innovation we have never ignored or taken for granted our inheritance. This insight lies at the heart of Philip's encounter with the eunuch. The central encounter of this story is a deep engagement with the pattern of God's love for creation as revealed in scripture. There is an open debate in New Testament scholarship as to whether the eunuch Philip met was a Jew or a Gentile (and for that matter whether he was a eunuch or merely a court official), but what is clear in the telling is that we are told that he knew scripture. It is the sight and sound of him reading the prophecy of Isaiah which prompts Philip to run alongside his chariot in the first place and engage him in conversation. Through the New Testament, and particularly in the book of Acts, we are reminded again and again that the good news of Jesus is not something new, but a consummation of the truth that God has unfolded in scripture. Peter on the day of Pentecost, Stephen before the crowd, and Philip to the eunuch—all begin with the tradition of scripture and from that show who God is in Jesus through this tradition.

This deliberate engagement with tradition is where God's Tent differs from other movements which seek to engage creatively with faith, spirituality and the landscape. In many of these it is common to contrast themselves with traditional church by beginning with creation as "the second book of God".[25] By contrasting themselves with inherited models of church these innovative approaches focus on the experience of God in the "thin-places" of the world, "where the spirit soars and we are lifted out of the everyday".[26] There is a deep value in this approach to the natural world as a spiritual resource. Living and working in the shadow of Hadrian's Wall I can testify to this truth, as Sunday by Sunday I will often see as many people parking their cars and putting on their walking boots to visit "their church" in the hills around us as I will find crossing the threshold of the churches I serve. God's Tent is, therefore, a response to this need. But it is a response to that experience which recognizes that if creation is the second book of God, scripture is the first. All our pitchings are based on and drawn from an engagement with scripture within the context of the liturgical year. This encounter with scripture is then experienced and understood through an engagement with the landscape in which we find ourselves pitched.

As God's Tent has developed, we have found again and again that the medium through which we make this engagement between God's revelation in scripture and creation comes through a new twist on traditional models of Christian spirituality. What we have learnt is that our worship and experience has rung most true when it has engaged with scripture, through the deep patterns and traditions of the worshipping life of the church, experienced and understood through a shared engagement with landscape and the natural world. So, we have used the structure of *lectio divina* to deepen a reading of the story of the wise and foolish builders by building dens and reflecting on this (chapter 10). Similarly, we have engaged with the decisive narrative of our faith in a scavenger hunt for *The Stations of the Cross* (chapter 8) and *The Stations of the Resurrection* (chapter 9). It would be flat-footed to try to read this three-fold pattern of scripture-tradition-creation into the story of Philip and the eunuch, but the essence of his missionary work remains: that we deepen our understanding of God when we place ourselves and our experience into the great story of God's love revealed in the person of Jesus Christ.

This conscious recognition of our inheritance not only informs the structure of the worship of God's Tent, but also the way in which it relates to the ongoing patterns of inherited worship in our parishes. If you wished, you could only encounter church through the monthly pitching of God's Tent. However, we work hard to "tether" God's Tent to the existing patterns of worship in our churches. We do this in two ways. The first is that God's Tent follows the same patterns and themes we follow in our children and family input, both in traditional Sunday School and Messy Church. This does not assume that families will attend all of these, but it means that there is a relationship between these patterns of worship in our church buildings and the pattern of worship we find in our pitching of God's Tent. The second is that we draw the themes of our children and family worship together in a monthly all-age service on a Sunday morning. Again, there is no assumption of compulsion, but there is a flow from one to the other. However, we have found that this linking of the innovation of God's Tent to our inherited patterns of church has been fruitful for both.

Getting out of the way

> When they came up out of the water, the Spirit of the Lord snatched Philip away; the eunuch saw him no more, and went on his way rejoicing.
>
> *Acts 8:39*

As we reflect on Philip's encounter with the Ethiopian eunuch, the final moment in their story might seem to be the hardest to connect to our experience. Although we have not (yet!) been plucked up and plonked down dozens of miles away as in Philip's case, we have found that the ability to get out of the way has been one of the most important things we have learnt. If the initial impetus for God's Tent was to engage older children, we soon learnt that its real power was in engaging people of all ages in conversations about faith. By making a creative activity central to the experience of our worship, God's Tent has created a space for conversations about faith and God to grow up naturally and organically. What we have found is that some of the most powerful conversations have happened when we, the leaders, have got out of the way. We have heard about conversations between new friends walking together as an activity is played out or between parents and children in the car on the way home. The joy of God's Tent has been that parents and children, young and old, have been able to talk to one another about God, and for that conversation to continue after we have packed up and gone home.

God's Tent fosters and encourages conversations and curiosity about faith which is not controlled or mediated by the leaders. In this way, there is an intrinsic equality in God's Tent. This might be because we sit in a circle on the floor; it might be because we are necessarily less formal in our style and clothing; it might be because of the unique, timeless and often anonymous space the tent creates as it is pitched in different locations each time. We will explore in more depth the role that the tent plays in creating and defining the space for worship and spiritual encounter in chapter 4. Whatever the reality of this is, we have found in God's Tent a new and exciting way of exploring faith. Above all things God's Tent connects us to that deep movement of God's mission we find not only in the book of Acts, but throughout scripture. God's Tent calls us to get out of our comfort zone and known environment, and draws us to the life of God's mission working out on the frontier that lies beyond us. Like Philip in his encounter with the eunuch, this could not have come unless we listened to the prompting of the Spirit, moved more quickly than we had expected, engaged with tradition and crucially got out of the way, so that we could all find God present in our midst, pitched among us.

CHAPTER 3

Pitched Among Us

To pitch a tent for worship is not just a pragmatic means of overcoming some practical problems. To pitch a tent for worship is explicitly to refer to one of the richest metaphors of divine presence available to us. All preachers know, as do a few weary Christmas congregations, that when John tells us in the prologue to his Gospel, "[a]nd the Word became flesh and lived among us" (John 1:14), the word we translate as "lived" (*skénoó*) derives from the word *skéné,* which means tent. So, when "the Word became flesh and *skénoó* among us", John is telling us that, in Jesus, "the Word became flesh and *pitched his tent* among us". This image places us in direct lineage with the rich theological image of a tent-pitching God, which draws us back through the language of John's prologue, through the establishment of David's kingdom to the promise and covenant of the Exodus and before.

Drawing on this image, this chapter is a theological reflection on the image of a tent-pitching God. Drawing on Terence Fretheim's *Interpretation* commentary on Exodus, this chapter will explore this metaphor.[27] Through this we can gather again the powerful picture of a God who dwells with his people, who orders their worship, who moves out in front of his people in mission, and who points us to the promised future for which we all hope. This is an image which is not limited to Exodus or John, but is a rich seam that runs through all of scripture, and which we are encountering in the God we are meeting in our pitching and re-pitching of God's Tent among us.

Coming down the mountain

"My presence will go with you, and I will give you rest."

Exodus 33:14

Through chapters 25–40 of the book of Exodus we are given a dramatic account of the creation, fall and re-creation not only of God's chosen people, but one of the fullest accounts we find in the Old Testament of the character and true nature of God who makes and redeems his people. The decisive moment in the process of divine self-revelation comes not in a proclamation, or a statement, but in movement. In this passage, we are told about the dramatic movement of God from the mountain-top down to his dwelling in the tent that he has pitched among his chosen people. Through the earlier chapters of Exodus we hear of Moses leaving the body of the people at God's command: "[c]ome up to me on the mountain" (Exodus 24:12). It is there that Moses speaks with God, there that God gives to Moses the tablets of the Law, and through this movement up and down the mountain that Moses stands as the mediator between God and his people. This is, after all, the pattern of relationship which would have been expected between the gods of the ancient world and their people. Like Zeus or Aphrodite (looking like Laurence Olivier and Ursula Andress) in flowing white robes looking down with benign disinterest at the lives of the mortals who worship them. This pattern of mountain-top worship is broken by the apostasy of the people through their casting and worshipping of a new god in the golden calf. Through Exodus 32–34 we hear of God's desire, in the role of a mountain-top god, to punish this sinful people from afar. But through Moses' intercession God takes another route. Rather than strike down his people, God comes down the mountain to be with them and, through God's presence, redeem them. As God says to Moses in response to his intercession, "My presence will go with you, and I will give you rest" (Exodus 33:14). Through this movement down the mountain we discover a God who does not remain removed from our experience. Instead we learn of the God who comes to dwell with his people. This is a God who does not judge or reject the messiness of his people's lives; this is a God who instead comes to dwell amongst them in the tent pitched in their midst.

This is a reality which we know all too readily in our pitchings of God's Tent. The experience is not a neat or controlled experience of church. It is, by its very nature, muddy and messy. We pitch in fields and woods where we get wet and muddy, where we fall over and get our hands dirty. This is not an experience of God reserved for our "Sunday best" but a way of getting to know who God is for us, where wellies and waterproofs are the norm not the exception. And this is not about getting muddy and messy for the sake of it, although this is often great fun. It is an experience and a way of getting to know God which acknowledges that our lives are often more like the messiness of our pitchings than they are the order and formality of our traditional worship. This is not to privilege this form of religious experience over the other. Rather it is to remind us that our God is one who comes down the mountain to be with us in this messiness, and in this we rejoice.

Sacred place

Moses used to take the tent and pitch it outside the camp.

Exodus 33:7

The vision of God we discover in these chapters of Exodus naturally grows from the God we learn about through the book of Genesis. Read in this context the decisive move of God "down the mountain" is not an aberration or a dramatic change, but the natural development of the God who, as we hear throughout the book of Genesis, comes close to his people and through that closeness reveals the holiness of these places of divine encounter. Through Genesis these moments are marked often by the building of an altar; the marking in stone and permanency the experience and promise of God revealed in that place. In Genesis 12, following God's call, Abram marks this first promise and covenant by "building an altar to the Lord who has appeared to him" (Genesis 12:7). In a similar way, in Genesis 28 we hear of Jacob's dream and of the ladder joining heaven to earth. Jacob marks this place of epiphany by taking the stone he had used as a pillow, anointing it and setting it up as a reminder that: "[h]ow awesome is this place. This is none other than the house of

God and this is the gate of heaven" (Genesis 28:17). Through Genesis we learn of a God who meets with his people in different times and places and the tradition of marking these places as sacred and holy. The movement of God down the mountain, to dwell with his people in the tent pitched for him, is therefore a development of this pattern of divine–human interaction where we know God not in an idea or principle but in a place and moment in time.

In the patterns of our inherited church we can internalize this experience of sacred place and encounter in a way which prioritizes the sacredness of the places we have inherited over the sacredness of the places in and through which we discover God's presence ourselves. So, for instance, God's Tent was first pitched and conceived in South Tynedale and in places redolent with the traditions of St Cuthbert and the community that carried his remains. In this context, as across the whole of those northern lands where—as the Anglo-Saxons called them—the *haliwerfolc* or "people of the saint" lived, the journey of Cuthbert and his community has created a sacred geography. The area stretching from the Scottish Borders to Ripon and the Northumberland coastline of Lindisfarne and Bamburgh to the west extremes of Dumfries is dotted with ancient churches dedicated to St Cuthbert, named because it is believed that Cuthbert's remains and the loyal community which surrounded him rested there for a time. They all created a sacred movement towards Cuthbert's final resting place and shrine at Durham.[28] So, in the Parishes by the Wall, we find ancient places of religious experience and encounter in St Cuthbert's Beltingham and Haydon Old Church, places where for centuries communities of faith have met and prayed and worshipped. In these places, like Jacob at Bethel, we have set up stones and anointed them and reminded ourselves and a forgetful world that these places are, in a small way, the house and gate of heaven. But alongside this inherited experience of sacred place we discover new generations of seekers who find the divine in the wonder of creation and the beauty of the landscape.[29] It would be easy to argue, and many in the Church do, that to reach this latter group of seekers we need to jettison some of the baggage of this inherited model of sacred place, and a good number of the buildings that we hold on to in this inheritance. In this argument, our buildings act as "transitional objects", things we hold on to for comfort, as we struggle to come to understand the nature of the new world and experience in which we are living. Our buildings, these ancient stones, do not enhance our experience of God; rather, they encumber our mission in the world.[30]

It would be tempting to see God's Tent as a means of innovation over and against the problems of this inheritance, and so become a way to remake our understanding of sacred place. Why, some might argue, do we need to meet God in a building when we can meet him in a tent? But this either/or argument is not what we have experienced through our pitchings of God's Tent. As we will see through this book, the pattern of God's Tent is to take many of the gifts we have inherited from the tradition of the Church and cast them in a new place and pattern. This way of thinking does not reject the old in favour of the new; rather, it finds new ways of encountering God in the patterns we have inherited from the old. The God who comes down the mountain in the book of Exodus is not a rejection of an old god in favour of a new, but the ever-flowing revelation of the God who walked "in the garden at the time of the evening breeze" (Genesis 3:8), who made his promise to Abram and Jacob, who responds to Moses' intercession and who comes to be with us in Jesus. As we pitch God's Tent, we are able to find God again and again in the world around us. The decisive move we learn of in this story, what Richard Giles has called "the Jewish religious genius", is that in coming down the mountain and dwelling in a tent God gives us a new concept of sacred space, where "God will come to his people on the move where they are".[31] So, as we pitch God's Tent we are not just meeting in familiar fields and favourite woods, in places of play and quiet contemplation. As we pitch God's Tent, we are able to remind ourselves that in these familiar places, and in a forgetful world, the Lord was and is and always will be in this place, and we did not know it.

The pattern of the tabernacle

"Have them make me a sanctuary, so I may dwell among them."

Exodus 25:8

God coming down the mountain to dwell with his people and to be close to them and the realities of their lives is not the beginnings of an overfamiliarity with God, like that moment when, in early adulthood, a former teacher suddenly suggests you call them by their first name. Far from it. In chapters 25–30 of Exodus, God narrates to Moses in minute detail the form and structure of the worship that will be brought to him in the sanctuary that they are to make for him. Detailing the exact dimensions and material for the sanctuary, the forms of sacrifice, the vestments for the priests, the patterns of daily worship, and the nature of the ritual cleanliness called for in the worship of this new sanctuary, God is bringing order to the worship of his chosen people. In the context of the book of Exodus, commentators have argued that these stringent codes of worship and ritual were a response to the lack of discipline and order of the multiple worship sites of the ancient world. We are given this insight through the dramatic tension built into this passage in Exodus. Like the cross-cutting of a highly wrought drama, we are encouraged to see the scenes play out simultaneously. In one frame we see Moses being given these ritual and liturgical instructions on the top of the mountain, as God prepares to descend to be with his people. In the other frame, at the foot of the mountain, the people of Israel are melting and casting their jewellery into a golden calf for their worship. The dramatic counterpoint of these two scenes only acts to highlight the importance of the former instructions in the face of the latter idolatry. Left to its own devices, and in the instability of the wilderness, humanity will worship anything; so structure, form and instruction is needed to bring stability and assurance in the uncertainty of this wilderness experience.

As stated in the previous chapter, God's Tent differs from other recent movements which engage creatively with the spiritual richness of creation. In the context of this insight from Exodus we can highlight two key threads to this difference. The first is that God's Tent is, in its physical form, a structured place of encounter in the landscape. We do not meet and gather under a tree or by a stream, but in a tent, in a place which we pitch, and form, and dwell in with God. This might seem like a trivial point, but it is a crucial aspect of what God's Tent is and can be. Our intention is not simply to find the divine in nature, but to use the richness of nature to discover God amongst us. This pattern of experience is mediated through the fact of the tent. This first insight leads to a second characteristic of God's Tent, which is that it is, in its entirety, an act of worship. Our worship may not be as ordered and proscriptive as that outlined for the worship God prescribes to Moses, but it is worship none the less. As we will see in the following chapters, the pattern of God's Tent is relaxed, but it has a structure. Each pitching follows the rough pattern of gathering with song and prayer, the sharing of and reflection on scripture through a creative activity, and a time of reflection and prayer. God's Tent is a time to have fun, to have conversations, to meet with friends in a new way, but we do this in and through the pattern of worship. As we noted in the last chapter, we have found that much of the strength of God's Tent comes from providing and creating spaces for families and people of all ages to meet with one another and God in a new way without those of us leading getting in the way. This space for encounter comes because of, not despite, the pattern of worship that frames our pitchings of God's Tent. It seems like such an obvious insight, but one which is worth stressing again, that our call as the Church is, above all things, to be a place of worship. In God's Tent we, like the people of ancient Israel in the wilderness, find God not by accident, but when we come to God in the forms and structures of worship that God sets before us.

God on the move

"I have been moving about in a tent and a tabernacle."

2 Samuel 7:6

It is God's initiative, detailed in Exodus, to come down the mountain, to dwell in a tent and to order humanity's encounter with God through worship. This divine initiative describes a God who is both intensive in the immediacy of our experience of God, and extensive in God's ongoing presence and movement through the lives and history of God's chosen people. As has already been stated, the closeness of God to our lives depicted in the pitching of the tent among us should not be mistaken for God creating a comfortable, localized and fixed experience of God's presence. Far from it. Beginning in the story of the Exodus, and then through the establishment of the nation of Israel, through to the calling of David as Israel's great king, we learn of a God who resists the attempts to limit and domesticate God. This is a God on the move, a God moving through the lives and history of God's people; this is a God on mission.

We find this nowhere more clearly than in the remaking of God's covenant with David in 2 Samuel 7. Walter Brueggemann has described this passage as "the dramatic and theological centre of the entire Samuel corpus".[32] It comes at the highpoint of David's kingship. Having defeated the Philistines, David has made Jerusalem his capital and, in scenes of intense joy and worship, David dances in front of the ark of the covenant as it is brought into Jerusalem. Having built himself a luxurious house of cedar, David tells the prophet Nathan that he will build an even more splendid home, a temple, for his tent-dwelling God. This offer is, though, not for the glory of God, but part of the process of legitimizing and normalizing David's new kingdom, bringing God's dwelling into the same domestic patterns as David's new palace. In the face of this offer God, through the prophet Nathan, reminds David of God's self-revelation through the story of the Exodus and beyond. As Brueggemann goes on to argue:

> The plushness of the proposed temple contradicts Yahweh's self-understanding. Yahweh will not be bought off, controlled, or domesticated by such luxury. Yahweh is a free God and will continue to be.[33]

God, Nathan tells David, does want David to build a house, but not of wood. God wants David to create a great house built in God's name: a house and kingdom which "shall be made sure for ever before me" (2 Samuel 7:16). However, as the narrative of Samuel–Kings moves forward, we discover that David's change of mind is not the final position. On taking the throne, David's son Solomon, forgetting Nathan's wisdom, succeeds in this earthly desire to domesticate this tent-dwelling God by building a temple (1 Kings 6:1–38). The establishment of the temple is, within the sweep of the story of God's people, a painful and provisional victory for Solomon and his successors. Richard Giles, in his seminal work, *Repitching the Tent*, goes so far as to see this as a moment of apostasy:

> Instead of God living in a tent, he was enshrined in a magnificent temple. Instead of his people encountering God alongside them on the road, they must now take the road to Jerusalem where he was to be found at journey's end. No longer did God pitch his tent among men.[34]

What the warning of Nathan and then the actions of Solomon show us is that the building of the temple and the domestication of God into a building removes from our understanding something of the essential character of God revealed in the image and story of this tent-dwelling God.

By pitching God's Tent for worship, we are, therefore, exploring and finding again a way of knowing and meeting God which we have lost sight of in some of the formality of our inherited worship patterns. Again, as with the discussion of sacred place, this should not be misread as an either/or between the value of tents over buildings as places of worship. As Brueggemann himself has pointed out, the form and order of the desert tent which we hear described in Exodus 26–31 was very likely refracted through the nearer memory of the Jerusalem temple in the imaginative remembering of the story of the Exodus.[35] In a similar way, as we explore this story, there is greater complexity in the relationship between the tent and the temple in the accounts of David and Solomon. If we compare the account of this story in 1 Chronicles to the narrative of Samuel–Kings, we find a much more explicit instruction from David to Solomon to build not only a great dynastic house, as we have seen in 2 Samuel 7, but a call from David for Solomon to construct a temple following the plans and using the resources David provided (1 Chronicles 22:2–19). This complexity between tent and temple lives on in our contemporary experience of this tradition when we remember that

Richard Giles' polemic in favour of "Repitching the Tent" is merely the call for the reordering of our inherited church buildings.

The ambition to find God in the pitching of a tent should not be read as a vain attempt to recreate and re-encounter a supposed authenticity of a wilderness faith in the face of the supposed "errors" of inherited patterns of worship. In the pitching of God's Tent we are articulating a truth which we often say, but seldom experience, that God's presence and activity is larger than some of the limits of our inheritance. In the context of the modesty and neatness of Anglicanism this might seem an uncomfortable truth to many. But we have found that God's Tent has become a simple means through which we can find and follow our God who has always been moving about amongst us in a tent. So, we have found that God's Tent is an easy way of working with colleagues across parish boundaries, where we don't have to have an uncomfortable argument about which building to meet in because we are gathering where God's Tent is pitched. Similarly, we can use God's Tent to engage with secular partners and friends like schools and community groups. This is not to try to "baptize" their spaces in a ham-fisted way, but to show that, subtly and quietly, God is at work in those places, and we can make that visible by pitching God's Tent among them.

God will be with them

He will dwell with them; they will be his peoples.

Revelation 21:3

Perhaps the most powerful aspect of the image and metaphor of the tent-pitching God is the future possibility that it reveals to us. In the fact of the tent that we discover in Exodus, in its practicality and provisionality, is a reality that it holds in it our present experience with the past that we bring to it, as well as the future that we look to in hope. As we have seen, through Genesis and Exodus we learn of a God who is not separate from our experience but who journeys with his people. God, through Nathan, emphasizes this again to David in 2 Samuel, reminding him that God has always lived and moved among his people in a tent. In the liturgical instructions in Exodus God remains constantly ready to move, when God forbids the removal of carrying poles from the ark of the covenant (Exodus 25:15). Even as the idea of God is domesticated in Solomon's temple the truth of God's restless, boundary-less movement persisted as the same carrying poles remained in place; ready and prepared to move again when required (1 Kings 8:8).

If the tangible reality of this was lost in the domestication of the temple the theological insight remained. As we remembered at the beginning of this chapter, it is this image of the tent-pitching God which John the Evangelist draws on to capture what God is doing in the incarnation: coming again, in the person of Jesus Christ, into the midst and messiness of the lives of his people to remake and redeem them as God did when he came down the mountain. So strong is this theological image that it is carried through to the very end of scripture where John the Divine, speaking at the end of his Revelation, draws from the same linguistic root that John the Evangelist uses when speaking of the incarnation (*skéné*) in his ecstatic vision of the new heaven and the new earth where God will dwell (*skēnōsei*), or pitch his tent, among his people in the new Jerusalem.

In the fact of the tent, in its constant movement, the taking down and putting up, the place and experience of God's presence is constantly made and remade, and through this process we glimpse the promise of God who creates and recreates in our midst. In the pitching and re-pitching of God's Tent, the past and future are held together in the reality and practicality and physicality of the tent. When we spread the tent out at the beginning of the pitching, we can find in it memories of the last pitching. Sometimes it is in the mud and mess of last time, sometimes in the leaves from the woods where we last pitched, sometimes in the hay we continue to pick out of the rugs gathered from our Christmas pitching in a stable alongside the animals on a working farm. Equally, as we gather up God's Tent at the end of our pitching, we are orientated to the future, capturing in prayer and shared experience the possibilities of what and where we will be next time God pitches his tent among us. These past memories and future possibilities are held together in the immediacy of the pitching which is, by its very nature, temporary and impermanent and "now". The promise of past, present and future is held together in and through the practical reality of our experience of God's Tent.

Part 2

CHAPTER 4

Getting Pitched

The purpose of this chapter is not to give a blueprint for how to pitch and establish the perfect God's Tent, if such a thing exists. Rather this chapter is the distillation of some practical and communal wisdom about how to establish and pitch God's Tent in your own context. For this reason, the chapter runs loosely in chronological order from the initial planning and acquisition of a tent, through the organizing and preparation, to the structure and pattern of the worship that frames each pitching of God's Tent. So, what follows does not ask so much "What do we need to do?" to pitch God's Tent, rather it asks "What do we need to be?" All the practical factors needed to establish your own expression of God's Tent need to be thoroughly discussed and agreed at a local level, and then used with a healthy dose of good sense and flexibility to recognize what will work and flourish in any given context. So these are not a set of strict rules; instead they are a set of helpful guides to capture the character and nature of God's Tent, and what others might do if they wish to pitch God's Tent among them.

. . . be hospitable

God's Tent should always be a place of hospitality, where those who gather feel that they are welcome. This is of course a truth which should be hard-wired into all experiences and expressions of church life. However, with God's Tent, as we are asking those who come to move figuratively and literally out of their comfort zone, it is important that what they experience is hospitable and welcoming. That does not mean that it needs to include all creature comforts, but it does mean that we need to work hard to ensure that we don't do things that make people feel uncomfortable, unwelcome or that this is not a space and place for them.

This focus on hospitality begins with the most obvious choice of all— the tent used as God's Tent. There is no real rule about which tent you might choose to purchase or borrow for this purpose, but there are some things which are worth bearing in mind as you begin. Choose something which is easy to put up, take down and pack away. There is no value in trying to create a space for worship and encounter if those doing it have spent the previous hour swearing under their breath as they deal with complex frames and ungovernable groundsheets. Similarly, it needs to be a space which is large enough for a reasonable number of people to gather. A small pop-up tent might be convenient to put up, but if you struggle to get two or three people in it, you will also struggle to meet one of Jesus' main characterizations of what it means to be a church.

We settled, after a good deal of research, on a six-metre bell tent. This has its limitations in that if it gets wet it can be time consuming to get the canvas fully dry. However, it is very easy to put up. Even in blustery conditions, in our experience, two fit people can get it up or down in twenty minutes. Ours also has two entrances, and the sides can also be rolled up on a warm day. Neither of these are essential to any of the pitchings we have done, but it has helped make it a more flexible space than one might initially think. The other thing about our bell tent is that it is an aesthetically pleasing thing in itself. It is worth remembering that in the chapters of Exodus on which we reflected in the last chapter there are long instructions on how the Tent of Meeting was to be a place of beauty. If we are meeting with God, doing it in an aesthetically pleasing space helps. Added to this, we have found that a bell tent has a certain timeless quality to it. It might hark back to memories of Enid Blyton or *Swallows and Amazons* or tap into the new fad for "glamping", but there is something about being in a tented space which has an ageless quality to it. Most of our tent is made from natural fabrics, and we have found that the organic colours of the canvas and carpets enhance the spaciousness and welcome the tent provides. As we think later on the value of being spacious in pitching God's Tent, it is important not to underestimate the value of doing this in a space that doesn't carry with it all the distractions of a modern tent which may support all the gadgets and gizmos of modern living.

Our bell tent cost us about £700, and with additional equipment we think we have spent about £1,000 getting established, which is not an inconsiderable investment for a small group of parishes. However, this investment has paid itself back several times over, not just in the development of God's Tent itself, but in the use of the tent as a space for parish and church events. So, we have pitched God's Tent at church fetes and community events, we are developing relationships with schools and we are lending it to another group of parishes developing God's Tent. Although the initial investment might seem prohibitive, we believe that it is an investment worth making and possible if local trusts, groups of parishes working together or wider church support are sought.

. . . be warm-hearted

The hospitality of God's Tent rests on more than the tent that is chosen. Whenever we prepare a space for worship, whether in a traditional church, in school for worship or in a tent, we are creating the best space that we can to come into God's presence. As already mentioned, we just need to look at the long and detailed instructions God gives to Moses and the Israelites in preparing the tent in the wilderness to recognize the value that has always been placed on making a space for worship, and make it as special as we can. While by its very nature we can't guarantee that God's Tent will be warm, we do think that it is possible to be a space which is warm-hearted. To do this there are certain things that are worth remembering.

In our experience, we can deal with most things that nature has to throw at us, but if you get cold it is hard to get warm again. Now, this does not mean that we can only pitch God's Tent in certain weather conditions, but it does mean that we can take a few helpful precautions. First, we always make a point in the week before we pitch God's Tent to let people know what we expect the weather to be like and so what clothing would be appropriate for the location. The second is that we try to ensure that the tent itself is as sheltered as it can be. Even on a cold day, with the doors closed, the tent can become quite cosy when everyone is inside. The third is to insulate the floor. A good rule of thumb is to try to have three layers between yourself and the bare earth. For us this is the ground sheet of the tent, then some coirmatting and then individual seating mats. These again add some value to the basic costs of God's Tent. For us, this was the additional £300 between the £700 for the tent and the £1,000 total cost. Most of this is for the coir matting which, although slightly bulky to store, makes a huge difference to the feel of the tent itself. We have also bought a number of foam kneelers designed for gardeners to act as insulating seating pads. These are not the most beautiful things, but they work well as individual cushions which might not make us warm but are very effective in ensuring that we don't get cold.

The second thing we do is spend some time making both the outside and inside of God's Tent beautiful. Working with local school children we have created some bunting based on our logo which we string up around the door. Inside we never use naked flames for obvious reasons, but we have found that LED "night-lights" and fairy lights are easily available to make the space more welcoming. We don't try to make God's Tent look like a traditional church, but we do work to make the space have a focus. As we use a bell tent, we have a small circular table which fits round the pole with three LED candles on it to provide a focus and centre to our worship.

The third thing is to consider the little things which make God's Tent feel hospitable and welcoming. Invariably we wear wellies when pitching God's Tent. We do, though, have one rule with God's Tent that you take off your shoes when coming in. This is partly because, like Moses approaching the burning bush, God's Tent is "holy ground". But it is also because we want to keep the mud on the outside of God's Tent. However, if you have ever regularly taken wellies on and off you will know that this is not always an easy procedure. So, we have bought an old rug and a welly-jack. It is just a small thing, but something to make it easier and more welcoming to be in God's Tent. Similarly, we always end God's Tent with simple hospitality, invariably hot chocolate. We don't make this part of the worship but have found it is a popular way to gather up, and warm up, at the end of the pitching before the work of tidying up commences.

. . . be adventurous

It is self-evident that an expression of church which is based on moving out into the landscapes of creation should be adventurous. However, when we have spoken to people about God's Tent it is often this factor, and worries about finding suitable places for pitchings, which seems to concern those who might be interested in pitching God's Tent in their own context. Their worries are that landowners might not welcome the intrusion and that public or semi-public spaces might not be available to them. Our experience is the complete opposite. Far from being concerned about God's Tent we have found it a productive way to engage and partner with landowners, public bodies and trustees of our shared landscape. So we have pitched God's Tent on the land of about half-a-dozen local farmers; on land owned or managed by the National Trust, the Northumberland Wildlife Trust, Northumberland National Park; in a local wood in the care of one of the civil parish councils; and on school and church grounds. At the time of writing there has never been an occasion when we have been refused permission to pitch God's Tent in a location we have chosen. In fact, we are getting to the stage now where some people are approaching us to ask if they can help.

Although developed in a rural context there is no reason why God's Tent could not be pitched and developed in urban contexts. The assumption would be that God's Tent is an idea that relies on the abundance of green open space which defines rural locations. But it would be wrong to think that these locations are the sole preserve of rural contexts. Even the most urban areas are filled with green spaces. Whether in formal parks or urban wild areas, all that is needed to pitch God's Tent is about eight to ten metres of green space, which is more available to us than we might imagine. In a recent study, the *UK National Ecosystem Assessment (NEA)* exploded the myth that we live in an interminably concreted and tarmacked country. While it is true that about 11 per cent of England is "urban", that means that nearly 90 per cent is not. But this figure does not mean that all of that urban landscape is covered in tarmac and concrete. *NEA* shows that 54 per cent of our towns is "greenspace"—parks, allotments, sports pitches etc., and that a further 25 per cent is made up of other non-built spaces—gardens, canals, reservoirs etc. That means that the proportion of England's total landscape which is built on is, according to *NEA*, 2.27 per cent.[36] It might need an imaginative leap to move the ideas of God's Tent from its initial rural setting, but it should not be impossible. The key, like all pitchings of God's Tent, is to be adventurous.

In finding places to pitch God's Tent we have followed a few simple rules. The first is to go initially to people that we know. God's Tent began in a context where local farmers and landowners are regular members of the congregations of the churches and so have been receptive to a request. Secondly, we have found it a good way to engage with public sector organizations such as the National Park or the National Trust. In urban contexts this might be the local council or schools. As long as we are sensible and flexible in our requests, we have found these groups very willing to accommodate us. Thirdly, we are always careful to ensure that we don't ask in a way or at a time which will get the wrong response. So, for instance, asking a sheep farmer for space during lambing is not usually very welcome. Similarly, we recognize that, based in parishes near Hadrian's Wall, there are areas of archaeological sensitivity where it is not possible or right to pitch a tent and drive tent-pegs into the ground. Fourthly, alongside this call to be adventurous is the need to be flexible and pragmatic. We have never had to cancel a pitching of God's Tent, although a Siberian blast came close once. We have managed this by being flexible and pragmatic. In the winter we try to pitch in places where there is a "plan B" so that if it is not practicable to pitch the tent we can gather and "pitch" in a barn or outbuilding. Sometimes we have done this by using a pop-up gazebo or event-shelter to create the space for us to gather in, but in a place and space which is not so limited by the weather.

. . . be safe

Alongside the call to be adventurous is the call to be safe. Pitching, exploring and worshipping in adventurous places naturally comes with risks and it is vital that those risks are always assessed, understood and managed. This focus on being safe works on three levels.

The first is that safety and awareness of risk was hard-wired into God's Tent from the beginning. From the outset, we spoke to our insurers to ensure that we were putting in place a robust structure, covered by our church's public liability insurance which should be part of a normal church insurance policy. As you come to define how you will pitch God's Tent in your own context you will need to ensure that you have made these arrangements yourself. Our experience is that insurance providers are very happy to discuss this with church groups in advance of any new venture and we would strongly recommend that you make this contact yourself in advance of your first pitching. In addition to this, we complete a risk assessment for every pitching we run. Some of the risks are regular and others are specific to that event. We ensure that this risk assessment, along with our public liability insurance certificate, is available to those whose land we are using in advance of the specific pitching. We also make sure that copies of the risk assessment are available at each pitching and explicitly in the hands of each of the leaders each time. In this first level we would also ensure that all those leading the pitching comply with the usual safeguarding protections we would expect to have in place for every church event, such as Disclosure and Barring Service (DBS) checks and appropriate safeguarding training. We also ensure that all who gather at God's Tent are kept safe by always following the up to date safeguarding policies of the benefice, diocese, and wider church. In addition, we would never have a pitching of God's Tent without a full and up to date first-aid kit which is at least British Standard (BS) 8599 compliant.

The second level is to ensure that the activities we do are appropriate to the ages of those gathered to the pitching. This means that if we are running an activity which carries with it a great risk, like the fire-lighting in the pitching outlined in chapter 7 for Christmas and Epiphany, we make sure that all the publicity stresses that this comes with a "PG" rating, and also that there is a parallel activity which would suit those for whom this "riskier" activity is not appropriate.

The third level is to stress through the pitching that looking after everybody is a shared responsibility. Central to God's Tent is the belief that this is something experienced by families together, and so we ensure that all children are in the care of a responsible adult (usually their parent). Secondly, we are explicit about where to explore during an activity, and also where not to explore, with these prohibited areas listed in the risk assessment. So, if we were pitched in a field with some sheep in it, by a river and close to some woods, we would explicitly say:

> For this activity we can go anywhere in this field, but be careful not to bother the sheep. There is no need to leave the field, unless you want to go into the woods at the far end, where we need to make sure we stay on the paths. If you are collecting something, be sure to collect things (sticks etc.) which have already fallen to the ground and not pulled off trees or picking wildflowers. There is no need for anyone to go anywhere near the river for this activity.

As with all things there is no way that we can remove risk from everything we do. But by being aware of these risks and managing them in a reasonable way we can ensure that God's Tent is safe for all who gather to it.

. . . be worshipful

At the heart of God's Tent is the highest vocation of all Christians, which is worship. God's Tent is, and should always be, an act of worship from beginning to end. The outline pitchings in the following chapters follow a simple recurring liturgical structure of *gathering, creating, reflecting* and *departing*.

Gathering

As we discussed in the previous chapter, in the Exodus the worship of the tent was to bring order and regularity to spiritual life. This worshipping pattern begins before people arrive in the space that has been created in the tent as described above, and as we enter God's Tent by taking our footwear off and recognizing that this is holy ground. This regular structure is, though, lightly held so that we don't need to be bound by books and words. Also, we use short, memorable and recurring responses to prayers. Music, if sung, is in the form of simply learnt repetitive chants and songs, and scripture copied out so that only those reading it need copies.

Each pitching begins with a gathering response which recognizes that in God's Tent we are tapping into that great tradition, both literal and figurative, of when God has pitched among us.

> When God led his people through the wilderness to the promised land . . .
> **God pitched his tent among us**
> When God made David a great king . . .
> **God pitched his tent among us**
> When God came to be with us in Jesus . . .
> **God pitched his tent among us**
> And today, here at [insert location] . . .
> **God pitches his tent among us.**

We then sing a short song. As you will see in the outline pitchings in the following chapters, these are often taken from "Wild Goose" resources from the Iona Community, Taizé, or simple refrains or choruses from well-known hymns and songs. There is no obligation to sing a song, or to sing a song from these sources, but we find that these short punchy chants are easy to teach and remember, can be sung unaccompanied if needed, and suit the feel of God's Tent.

Creating: Following a welcome, we share a reading from the Bible which will then act as the underpinning of that pitching. We use that reading as the basis for *creating* what follows. More often than not this activity takes us out of the tent into the spaces we have come to explore. As we do this, we are as clear and explicit as we can be about the nature of the activity and, as outlined above, what we need to be aware of to ensure that we are all kept as safe as possible.

When planning the *creating* we find it helps to be creative but also simple. By this we mean that often the longest part of the planning process is finding the right activity to help us explore the theme of that pitching. Some offer themselves—like fire-lighting in the depths of winter—but need care in the planning and organization. Others, like den-building for the wise and foolish builders, come from taking a creative leap from the exploration of the story into the activity used to understand it. The other thing we have found is the simpler and more straightforward the activity the better. Sometimes, as with scavenger hunts, this means not being overly proscriptive in what is asked for. Leaving space for those doing the *creating* to explore, wonder and make their own minds up is more important than finding what we might think to be just the right thing. On other occasions, asking people to do one thing well offers more time and space for personal reflection and conversation.

This last point leads to an important factor in planning and organizing the *creating*. One of the key objectives of the *creating* is to make it spacious. In this way, it must be remembered that the activity is not a break in the worship, but an essential part of it. In chapter 2, we discussed how part of the character of God's Tent, reflecting on the story of Philip and the Ethiopian eunuch, comes when the leaders actively remove themselves from the conversations and allow those gathered—very often parents and children—to explore and reflect together. This theme of spaciousness links with the seemingly timeless aesthetic of God's Tent, where it is possible to give people the time to walk and talk and reflect in a structured but not hurried way. At a time when family life is so often marshalled and organized minute by minute, having time as a family to hunt for "just the right stick", and discuss why they think it is "just the right stick" for the story or reflection we are exploring together is priceless.

Reflecting: At the end of the *creating* we gather again to reflect on what we have learnt with one another. At this point the role of the leader is to ensure that this *reflecting* is appropriate to the group gathered at that time and in that place. In the outline pitchings in the following chapters it is assumed that this gathering will be for a mixed group of children and adults. However, I can think of occasions when we have pitched God's Tent and only had adults and teenagers gathered to it. On that occasion the response, which was designed to be quite general, turned into a deeper conversation about what each person had discovered and recognized in the *creating*. On another occasion we gathered as a group of parents and early-years aged children. Here the *reflecting* had to be changed to something much simpler than planned, focusing on a simple and memorable way of taking away the key idea we were exploring in that pitching. As you pitch God's Tent and get to know those who are gathering to it better, you will learn to think on your feet so that the gathering-again and reflection time suits the needs of those gathered to God's Tent.

Departing: This time of *reflecting* is then brought together into a time of prayer. Again, there is no fixed way that this prayer should happen. Sometimes the prayer fits well when it is weaved into and through the reflection. So if you are exploring the Stations of the Cross then, as you reflect on each of the stations and the objects collected to help us understand that part of the story, it is fitting, and in keeping with the spiritual practice of that tradition, to gather each station up in prayer. On other occasions the prayers will flow out of the reflection time, as people share what they have found and learnt. On other occasions the prayer will come as a gathering up at the end of the *reflecting*.

As you develop your own understanding and expression of God's Tent you will find patterns of prayer that flow naturally from the *reflecting*. The main thing is that there is prayer. We would then always gather that prayer together with the Lord's Prayer, and a final song before closing with a final prayer of blessing which mirrors the gathering prayers and points us towards the next pitching of God's Tent.

> May God the Father walk with us as we leave his tent.
> May God the Son live in us as we return to our homes.
> May God the Holy Spirit guide us as we walk through life,
> till we gather again, in God's Tent, pitched among us. **Amen.**

. . . be together

As the vicar of two small parishes in rural Northumberland, I have always taken great comfort from the fact that Jesus does not say a great deal in the Gospels about what a church should be. However, he does say that there should be at least "two or three" (Matthew 18:20) and it should be "salt" and "light" (Matthew 5:13–16). God's Tent is never going to be big; if it was, it would lose the character of what makes it God's Tent. But by its very nature we have found that it is a fruitful way for small groups of people to be salt and light for one another. In this way, God's Tent gets its character not just from the tent you choose, or from the pattern or shape to the worship and activity you follow, but from the community that is created in and through it. God's Tent becomes something that those who are part of it help to create. This is literally the case as we all work together to put up and take down the tent, from the youngest collecting the tent pegs, to the eldest serving and tidying the hot chocolate. It is in this interaction, in these spaces around the spaces, that the true value of God's Tent is found, and in that ongoing community God's presence remains with us even when the tent is packed away and drying out for another month.

CHAPTER 5

Becoming Church

This session works well as the first "pitching" you might have of God's Tent. Firstly, because it helps establish some ownership of the tent as a place of gathering and worship as you will literally be putting up and reflecting on the tent itself in this session. Secondly it can work well in a familiar place near a church—most obviously a churchyard. If you are drawing together people unfamiliar with church, or perhaps a little unsure about what God's Tent is, having the first pitching in a familiar place can help.

The session itself has two parts. The first is the process of putting up the tent. With a new group this helps everyone get familiar with the tent, to make it something they are all a part of, from the oldest to the youngest. In our experience, even the smallest children can help with counting out the tent pegs and decorating the tent, even if some of the heavy lifting has to be left to the older members of the group. By getting everyone involved in this very practical act everyone can have ownership of the tent as their space and place to be with each other and God.

The second part of the session is reflection on and praying for the different parts of that pitching. This reflection on the parts of the tent and the ways in which it speaks of God's story with us reflects many of the ancient liturgies and traditions around the consecration of churches or the blessing of homes. As you will see below, there is no formal order to this, although there is a sort of natural flow which you will follow, beginning with the ground you chose. The central message is to reflect on and pray for the tent, not just as a thing, but as a sign or symbol—a sacrament even—of God's presence with us and who, in Jesus, is pitched among us.

Where to pitch the tent

As already suggested, we found this session worked well in the churchyard of our parish church. This is already a space which is used for church events like the summer fete and so we could use this space easily. There are, in many churches and communities, understandable sensitivities about having a session like this in a churchyard, especially if it is currently used, or has recently been used, as a burial ground. Also, there are often good practical reasons why a churchyard may not be suitable, particularly if there is not an obvious open space or worries about the safety of headstones, memorials or trees. If, on balance, a churchyard is not the most suitable place, then somewhere in clear sight of an existing church helps with the deep message of this session; that in pitching God's Tent we are making a church, not just in the thing we are making—the tent—but in the community we are becoming, as the *ecclesia*, as those God has gathered in God's presence.

What will you need (beyond the normal)

You will not need anything beyond the tent and accompanying equipment and additions that you might have. This is, though, a chance to make it your own, and so think beyond the basics to things that will make it feel like a special place marked out for you to be with each other and God:

- Perhaps fairy lights, battery tealights (avoid anything with a naked flame!).
- We have also created and decorated bunting flags. These could be decorated during the session, or perhaps some decorated in advance of this session and then put up by those who decorated them.
- There are also two suggested songs you might like to sing. If so, you might need to have the words prepared and some means of accompanying the singing.

What you might need to think of to keep everyone safe (beyond the normal)

At every pitching of God's Tent we need to be aware of hazards in the area where you are pitching. In this case you should take particular care if in a graveyard around headstones, memorials and trees.

The Pitching

GATHERING (AND CREATING)

Have the tent and all the things you need for the session piled up on the edge of the space you have chosen for the pitching. When you think everyone is there, begin very informally. Work together to find a spot and put up the tent bit by bit. Make sure everyone is involved in doing this, but don't say too much about what you are doing or why. Just focus on working together to pitch the tent. When it is all finished then gather in the tent and begin. It doesn't matter if this takes a long time; in reality, this is the main activity undertaken in this session. The only thing to remember is to take your shoes off before entering the tent together.

Song suggestion: 'Come, all you people' (Uyai mose) by Alexander Gondo, in John L. Bell, *Come All You People: Shorter Songs for Worship* (Glasgow: Wild Goose Publications, 1994).

Opening Prayer: If this is the first time you have pitched God's Tent, then you will need to introduce people to the opening prayers and the shared responses.

> When God led his people through the wilderness to the promised land . . .

Welcome: You can use this as a script or as a guide to introduce the session.

> Today we are thinking about what it means to be a church. If I was to ask you where the church is, what might you say?

You might get responses pointing to the church building, or to the tent, or to the people—the key is that all the answers are right.

> In putting up this tent together we have made a church, made a place where we can be with each other and God. There is a tradition of blessing buildings that are to become churches, and blessing people's homes and workplaces to help us remember God's presence in that place. What we're going to do is to think about the things we do to make this our church and our place and give thanks to God for that.
>
> So, what did we do?

REFLECTING

The following headings do not have to be taken in order (although they are in the order followed when we did this pitching), and there might be steps missed out or other ones added in. The key thing is to focus on the actions we did, to focus on the scripture, to talk about this a little, and to give thanks.

1. Finding the ground

Begin with a reading, perhaps sharing them among the group:

> The Lord said to Abram, after Lot had separated from him, "Raise your eyes now, and look from the place where you are, northwards and southwards and eastwards and westwards; for all the land that you see I will give to you and to your offspring for ever."
>
> *Genesis 13:14–15*

Then ask these, or similar open questions for discussion:

- Why did we choose this ground?
- What made it the right place to choose?
- What are we thankful for in this ground we have?

This could be brought together in silence or simple prayer like this:

> Loving God, you promised Abram a land to live in and prosper. Thank you for this place and ground you have given us to be with you. **Amen.**

2. Pegs

Reading:

> Thomas said to them, "Unless I see the mark of the nails in his hands, and put my finger in the mark of the nails and my hand in his side, I will not believe." A week later his disciples were again in the house, and Thomas was with them. Although the doors were shut, Jesus came and stood among them and said, "Peace be with you." Then he said to Thomas, "Put your finger here and see my hands. Reach out your hand and put it in my side. Do not doubt but believe."
>
> *John 20:25–29*

Suggested question:

- What happened on the cross?
- Why were the nails important?
- What marks do we carry?

Possible prayer:

> Father God, your Son carries the marks of the nails on his body to show his love for us. May we share all of ourselves with those who we meet in your name. **Amen.**

3. Pole

Reading:

> [Jesus] led them out as far as Bethany, and, lifting up his hands, he blessed them. While he was blessing them, he withdrew from them and was carried up into heaven.
>
> *Luke 24:50–51*

Suggested questions:

- Did the story of Jesus end on the cross?
- What happened next?
- How are we drawn to heaven?

Possible prayer:

> Loving God, in your Son Jesus, heaven and earth meet. May our prayers in this place bring us closer to the worship of you in heaven. **Amen.**

4. Doors

Reading:

> [Then Jacob said,] "How awesome is this place! This is none other than the house of God, and this is the gate of heaven."
>
> *Genesis 28:17*

Possible questions:

- What does it mean for somewhere or something to be "awesome"?
- What does it mean to worship?
- How could this tent be the gate of heaven?

Suggested prayer:

> God of Israel, you showed Jacob a vision of heaven. May our worship in this place bring heaven and earth together. **Amen.**

5. Carpets/Tables/Decoration

Reading:

> Let mutual love continue. Do not neglect to show hospitality to strangers, for by doing that some have entertained angels without knowing it.
>
> *Hebrews 13:1–2*

Possible questions:

- How do we make people feel welcome?
- How might we use this tent as a place of welcome?
- What does it mean to welcome people in Jesus' name?

Suggested prayer:

> God of welcome, you welcome each of us as your children and friends. Help us welcome others to this tent in your name. **Amen.**

6. Each other

Reading:

> [Jesus said,] "Truly I tell you, if two of you agree on earth about anything you ask, it will be done for you by my Father in heaven. For where two or three are gathered in my name, I am there among them."
>
> *Matthew 18:19–20*

Possible questions:

- Could any of us have done this alone?
- What else can't we do alone?
- What happens when we work together?

Suggested prayer:

> Creator God, you made each one of us in your image. May we find in each other your Spirit revealed in your Son Jesus here among us. **Amen.**

7. Take off our shoes

Reading:

> God called to [Moses] out of the [burning] bush, "Moses, Moses!" And he said, "Here I am." Then he said, "Come no closer! Remove the sandals from your feet, for the place on which you are standing is holy ground."
>
> *Exodus 3:4–5*

Possible questions:

- In what places do we take off our shoes?

- Why do we take off our shoes?
- How do we know this is a special place?

Suggested prayer:

> God of Moses, you revealed yourself in the burning bush. May
> we recognize you in the burning beauty of your creation. **Amen.**

DEPARTING

Song suggestion: 'Let us build a house' by Marty Haugen.

Prayers: (changing voices, if possible for each paragraph).

> May God give his blessing to his tent.
> God bless this ground, the pegs, the sheet.
> God bless the frames, the poles, the doors.
> God bless our seats, our places, each other.
> God bless its foundation and its covering.
>
> We call upon the Sacred Three
> to save, shield, surround
> this place, this tent, this community.
>
> May all be welcomed here
> friend and stranger, from near and far.
> May each be blessed and honoured as they enter.
>
> Peace be here in the name of the King of life
> the peace of Christ above all peace;
> the Lord's blessing over all.

Adapted from "A house-blessing" in *Celtic Daily Prayer: Book One—
the journey begins*, Northumbria Community Trust (London: William
Collins, 2015).

The Lord's Prayer

Final Prayer:

May God the Father walk with us as we leave his tent . . .

CHAPTER 6

Rejoicing in Creation—
Praying the Rainbow

One of the most vibrant and easily recognizable images from scripture is the image of the "bow in the clouds" (Genesis 9:13). More often than not this picture of the rainbow is accompanied by a cheery image of a smiling Noah, with his smiling wife and smiling animals as they bob around the waters of the flood in their boat. However, this picture is more complicated and rich than the understandable, but naive, version of Noah and the rainbow that we find in many children's books. In the context of this story the rainbow is a sign of God's renewed promise and covenant with humanity and creation. It is also a sign of hope as Noah and his family begin the task of beginning again after the devastation of the flood had subsided. It is not only a sign of hope for that generation, but a sign of ongoing hope and commitment for all creation: "The sign of the covenant that I make between me and you and every living creature that is with you, for all future generations" (Genesis 9:12). The rainbow is also a symbol of the whole breadth and wealth of creation. Ecologists have looked to the rainbow as a symbol for the richness of creation, and to the covenant for which it stands as a covenant not simply between God and humanity, but between God, humanity and all of created order.[37] There is, therefore, a spiritual richness in the image of the rainbow which draws us not simply to God's covenantal promise but to reflect on and give thanks for creation.

One of the sources for the spiritual richness of the image of the rainbow comes from an unusual source: the writings of Sir Isaac Newton. We owe our understanding of the seven colours of the rainbow to Newton's experiments on light and optics from the late seventeenth century. In these Newton showed, by passing light through a prism, how the colour spectrum is revealed in the refraction of white light, rather than a mixture of light and dark as had been thought previously. Newton, who we now recognize not simply as a scientist but also as a man of profound if unorthodox religious belief, saw deep spiritual resonances in this discovery. In particular, it has been argued by some that Newton made a deliberate analogy, following Kepler's belief in the doctrine of harmonies, between the seven colours of the rainbow and the seven notes of the musical scale, the harmony of the latter providing a counterpart to the harmonious form of the former.[38] Whatever the origins of our understanding of the rainbow, it continues to be a powerful means through which we celebrate the variety and vibrancy of humanity and creation. This pitching, and its celebration of this traditional sevenfold form, is just one means of responding to the harmony of creation.

Where to pitch the tent

The original inspiration for this pitching came from a desire of a colleague to pitch God's Tent near the wildflower hay meadows which are a feature of the high pastures of Northumberland during the summer months. The meadows, with their riot of wildflower and colour, are a wonderful space to look for and explore the breadth and colour of creation. Increasingly, local councils are planting wildflowers in verges and common areas and you might have one of these near you. Similarly, this pitching would work in the autumn with the variety of colours which characterize that season. The main thing is to find the right time of year and location where it is possible to hunt for this variety of colour around us.

What will you need (beyond the normal)

This is a simple pitching which involves searching and discovering things to represent these different colours. As we will see, the activity in the *creating* is not to *collect*, but to *record* what we find. There are two reasons for this. The first is that because many wildflowers and fungi are rare, it is illegal to pick them. Although not all the things we discover will be rare it remains a good rule of thumb not to pick any wildflowers. The second is that some things of vibrant colour can also be toxic and even poisonous. So, by recording and not picking anything we are ensuring that we protect both ourselves and the nature we have come to enjoy. For this reason, you will need to provide a means of recording what is discovered. This might be by preparing a sheet listing the colours of the rainbow with space for pictures to be drawn along with packs of colouring pencils. Another option is to use a mobile phone camera to record what is found. The main thing is to have a record of the variety of things found for the reflection.

What you might need to think of to keep everyone safe (beyond the normal)

The only possible unseen hazard in this task is in the naturally occurring poisons and toxins of some wild plants. A good nature guidebook is helpful in these circumstances to identify unknown plants that might be discovered.

The Pitching

GATHERING

Song suggestion: 'Heaven and Earth' in John L. Bell, *Come All You People: Shorter Songs for Worship* (Glasgow: Wild Goose Publications, 1994).

Opening Prayer:

> When God led his people through the wilderness to the promised land . . .

Welcome: You can use this as a script or as a guide to introduce the session.

> Today we are thinking about the whole wonderful variety and vibrancy of creation. We are going to think about this through the story of Noah. Who can help us tell the story of Noah?

Allow the group to work through the story of Noah in their own words, leading to the final story of the rainbow and the covenant. If the group doesn't quite get to this part of the story—sometimes we get to dry land and stop—the following Bible reading can be used to draw this telling of the story together.

Reading:

> Then God said to Noah and to his sons with him, "As for me, I am establishing my covenant with you and your descendants after you, and with every living creature that is with you, the birds, the domestic animals, and every animal of the earth with you, as many as came out of the ark. I establish my covenant with you, that never again shall all flesh be cut off by the waters of a flood, and never again shall there be a flood to destroy the earth". God said, "This is the sign of the covenant that I make between me and you and every living creature that is with you, for all future generations: I have set my bow in the clouds, and it shall be a sign of the covenant between me and the earth. When I bring clouds over the earth and the bow is seen in the clouds, I will remember my covenant that is between me and you and every living creature of all flesh; and the waters shall never again become a flood to destroy all flesh. When the bow is in the clouds, I will see it and remember the everlasting covenant between God and every living creature of all flesh that is on the earth". God said to Noah, "This is the sign of the covenant that I have established between me and all flesh that is on the earth."
>
> *Genesis 9:8–17*

CREATING

In introducing the *creating* you will want to talk about the different colours that make up the rainbow. This might be in bringing in some of the information about Isaac Newton outlined above, if that is appropriate for the group. It might simply be that you remind people of, or teach them, the rhyme, "Richard of York gave battle in vain", to remember the colours. You might also like to use this script to set out the task and clarify the parameters:

> At the heart of God's promise or covenant is the sign of the rainbow as a means of reminding us of God's care, and our responsibility, for all of creation. What we are going to do now is explore that creation and find and record things which represent all the colours of the rainbow. To do this you don't need to pick any of the flowers or other coloured things you might find. It would not be very responsible of us to enjoy God's creation by simply picking bits of it. Rather we want you to record what you discover either with a picture or a photograph. Seven different things that represent the seven colours of the rainbow—Red, Orange, Yellow, Green, Blue, Indigo and Violet.

REFLECTING

The structure of the *reflecting* is governed by the colours of the rainbow. Reflecting on each colour in turn and sharing what we discovered and recorded for that colour, we can reflect on what that colour might represent. Each group will find a different answer to these questions but offered below are the suggestions we came up with, with a short prayer to gather up these times of reflecting. Feel free to follow this pattern or follow your own themes and write and pray your own prayers following the themes you discover together.

1. Red: Blood and Life

Faithful Jesus, in the blood of the cross you show us the way to eternal life. We pray for those whose blood is still spilt in our world today, that your love and care would guide them to peace. **Amen.**

2. Orange: Sun and warmth

Father God, on the second day of creation you made the warming light of the sun. Thank you for the life that that brings to all creation. **Amen.**

3. Yellow: Celebration

Gracious God, thank you for the times we celebrate with you and one another. May our rejoicing mirror the rejoicing of heaven. **Amen.**

4. Green: Growth and creation

Creator God, we thank you for the abundance of your creation. May we share it with others, as you share it with us. **Amen.**

5. Blue: Water and Baptism

God of Life, in the blue water of baptism we find new life in your love. May the water of all creation quench and sustain our thirsty world. **Amen.**

6. Indigo (Purple): Power and Authority

Just God, we pray for all who exercise authority in our world. May they know and live by the power of your just and gentle rule. **Amen.**

7. Violet (Pink): Love

> God of love, thank you for the gift of love revealed in your Son.
> As we care for your creation, may we love it as you love us. **Amen.**

DEPARTING

Song suggestion: 'For yours is the kingdom' in John L. Bell, *Come All You People: Shorter Songs for Worship* (Glasgow: Wild Goose Publications, 1994).

The prayers of the *reflection* should gather up the prayers for this pitching, but offering time for final reflection and prayer as you prepare to depart is always helpful. This is then gathered up in the Lord's Prayer and ending.

The Lord's Prayer

Final Prayer:

> May God the Father walk with us as we leave his tent . . .

CHAPTER 7

Light in the Darkness

It is no coincidence that Christians celebrate the seasons of Advent, Christmas and Epiphany at the darkest point of the year. Although we don't know exactly when Jesus was born, it is perfectly logical that the first Christians, gathered in the northern hemisphere of the world, found that point of the year, just after the winter solstice when we turn from darkness to light, as the most evocative time to understand the coming of Jesus, the light of the world. Anthropologists of religion will remind us that many of the Christian festivals and traditions of this season share with similar festivals from other religious traditions, but that should not change the power Christians find in experiencing the coming of the light at the darkest part of the year.

In this pitching we think about the coming of the light into the world in a very real and practical way by kindling a light and building a fire. By doing this we are tapping into something deep within ourselves, that when things are dark and cold (and probably wet) we want to find the light and gather around it. More than this, the process of trying to create a flame with our bare hands, not with matches or a lighter, reminds us how fragile a light can be. But also, as we nurture that light and help it grow, how powerful and warming and uplifting this can be for us. As the pitching concludes, the experience of standing around the fire in the darkness (perhaps with a toasted marshmallow or s'more!) provides a wonderful opportunity to talk about and reflect on St John's great words that "the light shines in the darkness, and the darkness did not overcome it" (John 1:5).

Where to pitch the tent

As this pitching is designed for Christmas and Epiphany, you will be potentially fighting against some of the wildest weather of the year. For this reason, somewhere sheltered, with a good space to kindle and develop the flames (which will then grow into a larger fire) away from the tent is a good idea.

What will you need (beyond the normal)

You will be kindling a flame using a flint and steel. These are easily available for a few pounds from outdoor shops or online. Along with the flint and steel you need:

- Foil trays to get your fire started.
- Cotton-wool (teased out to catch the sparks from the flint and steel).
- Dry twigs and leaves to begin to build the flame.
- Dry kindling and firewood to build the central fire.
- A fire-pit or old barbeque to make the central fire.
- Fire extinguishers and safety equipment.
- Holding candles.

What you need to keep everyone safe (beyond the normal)

This is certainly an activity which carries with it some risk. You will need to think carefully about where this is to happen to ensure you have the permission of the landowner to light fires. At a minimum you will need to:

- ensure that children are supervised by adults at all times.
- ensure that everyone is aware of their own responsibility to keep themselves and everyone else safe.

- ask one of the adults to act as a "fire marshal", who is in charge of ensuring that the activity of making and growing the fire is safe at all times.

The Pitching

GATHERING

Song suggestion: The chorus of 'Christ be our Light', by Margaret Rizza.

Opening Prayer:

> When God led his people through the wilderness to the promised land . . .

Welcome: This is a script you might like to use or alter for your own purposes.

> January is a rubbish time of year. Christmas seems a long time ago. It is cold and dark and wet, and it doesn't seem that the weather will get warmer or the days any lighter. It is, as C. S. Lewis said about Narnia, "always winter and never Christmas".
>
> Except that it is still Christmas. We are in the season of Epiphany when we remember the sharing and revelation of the Jesus child to the whole world. We know this through the story of the Three Wise Men which was an epiphany or shining out of God's love in Jesus to the world. This gift is often described as the light of the world and we are going to think about, experience and reflect on that light today.
>
> This is how St John, at the beginning of his Gospel, tells us about Jesus, the light of the world.

Reading:

> In the beginning was the Word, and the Word was with God,
> and the Word was God. He was in the beginning with God. All
> things came into being through him, and without him not one
> thing came into being. What has come into being in him was
> life, and the life was the light of all people. The light shines in the
> darkness, and the darkness did not overcome it.
>
> *John 1:1–5*

> We are going to make a light, and then a flame, and then a fire.
> As you do this, think about how precious this light is, how much
> work you need to do to kindle and protect the light. And then
> as we finish think about how different it feels for us, in the dark
> and cold and the wet, to gather around that light.

CREATING

The core of this session is the kindling and building of a fire. It is worth
trying this out in advance of the pitching to ensure you know how to do
this and there are several easy online tutorials available if you search the
internet for "flint and steel". Below is a method which we have used and
found effective.

1. Split into small groups, always with a responsible adult in charge.
2. If possible, gather up some twigs and dry leaves to help with the
   kindling of the flame.
3. Tease apart some of the cotton wool and place in the foil tray. If
   you like, dip some of the cotton wool in petroleum jelly to make
   a simple wick and wax candle; this helps the cotton wool burn
   longer and gives you more chance of getting your fire started.
4. Use the flint and steel to create the sparks to light the cotton wool
   close to where the fire pit or barbeque will be used for the central
   fire.

5. Once lit, use the collected twigs and leaves to slowly build the fire. Be careful though; if you build too quickly you will put the fire out.

6. Build slowly using larger pieces of sticks and possible kindling. When the fire in your foil tray is well established carefully carry to the central fire and add it to the other groups' fires to build a bigger fire.

7. Once all the groups' fires are collected together, start to add larger pieces of wood to build into a more substantial fire.

Once the central fire is established, enjoy taking time to watch the fire grow. Enjoy feeling the heat and warmth of this new light in the darkness. With adult supervision, you might like to make hot chocolate or s'mores, or toast marshmallows on the fire. This then becomes a wonderful space for a gathering again and a conversation.

REFLECTING

As everyone is enjoying the fire and the refreshments, this is a chance to ask again and build a conversation again on these, or similar, questions.

- How hard was it to kindle and protect the light you made?
- What did that feel like?
- What was easy?
- What was hard?
- How different does it feel to be here with this light shining in the darkness?
- What can we do to kindle, and protect, and grow the light of the world in our lives and world?

As the conversation develops and concludes, ask someone to read again the passage from the beginning of John's Gospel. As this is done, hand round the holding candles and light them from the fire.

DEPARTING

Song suggestion: 'The Lord is my light' by Jacques Berthier, *Taizé Community.*

Prayers: You might like to use this or another prayer to gather together your prayers.

> Lord Jesus Christ,
> light of the nations and glory of Israel:
> make your home among us,
> and present us pure and holy
> to your heavenly Father,
> your God, and our God.
>
> *Church of England Collect for Candlemas*

The Lord's Prayer

Final Prayer:

> May God the Father walk with us as we leave his tent . . .

CHAPTER 8

Stations of the Cross Scavenger Hunt

The Stations of the Cross are an ancient and integral part of the observance of Lent for millions of Christians. Many churches in the catholic tradition have the traditional fourteen Stations of the Cross—nine scriptural and five based on traditional devotion—on the walls of their churches. The practice of walking these stations, reading scripture, pausing and praying is a powerful way of engaging actively with the path that Jesus walked for all of us in the first Holy Week. It is believed that the devotion grew from the desire of early Christians to follow the path that Jesus walked in their visits to Jerusalem, stopping and praying at those points in that journey that are spoken of in the Bible. Although there are now traditionally understood to be fourteen stations, the numbers have varied over the years. For this session we have focused on seven of the scriptural stations. The structure is very simple, and you might like to adapt, change or add to those which you use. The key, though, is that we are all, in this pitching, encouraged to walk these stations, to discover something through them, and in that to understand more the path of suffering that Jesus walked for each of us.

This pitching, and the one that follows—The Stations of the Resurrection—take the form of a scavenger hunt. We have used this activity on several occasions, not just in these two sessions. We have found that it is an effective way of inviting those gathered at that pitching to find their own personal response to the question being asked, in this case finding their own objects which speak to them of the different stations. This means that everyone's response and experience will be different. We have found this to be a helpful way of sharing simply our different experiences and responses to faith. The only exceptions are the one or two objects that are placed for people to find—however, even then we find that people experience these in different ways.

Where to pitch the tent

For scavenger hunts you need to find a location which has as much variety as possible. We have found that in and around woodlands can be really good places to pitch. This means that there is a variety of places to explore and discover different things. There is always a danger that some people will collect the first thing that they see and so whip through the activity too quickly. This is where the two pre-prepared objects help, in this case coins and strips of cloth, as they can be placed at some distance from the tent, or in places which are more difficult to find, to encourage people to search thoroughly. It is, though, advisable to have someone from the leadership team to be near these objects to help people find them if they are struggling.

What will you need (beyond the normal)

- Copies of the Stations including the Bible readings. You might like to laminate them to make them waterproof and reusable.
- A copy of pictures of traditional Stations of the Cross.
- Small bags to collect things in.
- Two pieces of string per person.
- A bowl of coins (we bought some plastic "silver" coins from a toy shop).
- A basket of strips of white cloth.

What you might need to think of to keep everyone safe (beyond the normal)

- When setting people off on an activity which they should follow, it is important to be clear where the boundaries are. So, when running scavenger hunts we have been clear to say that "You won't find anything beyond the bridge" or "Please do not leave the paths in the woods". This will of course change with the location that you choose, but setting the boundary helps people know where to go and where to look.
- Alongside this, we have found it best to tell people to keep to the paths. It is fun to explore, but this can add to the risk. There is nothing people will be asked to look for that you would not be able to find alongside the already existing paths and byways of a place you will be exploring.
- It is also helpful to be clear where, in general terms, the placed items are (i.e. at the highest point of the path etc.) so that people search but don't get lost!
- On scavenger hunts we also set a few basic rules for people to follow:
  - Only collect things which are already on the ground.
  - Don't cut or break anything.
  - Don't pick any wildflowers.

The Pitching

GATHERING

Song suggestion: 'Stay with me', Taizé.

Opening Prayer:

> When God led his people through the wilderness to the promised land . . .

Reading:

> Then Jesus told his disciples, "If any want to become my followers,
> let them deny themselves and take up their cross and follow me.
> For those who want to save their life will lose it, and those who
> lose their life for my sake you will find it."
>
> *Matthew 16:24–25*

Introduction: You might like to use this script or adapt the meaning into your own words:

> We are in Lent. This is the time in the Church year when we
> prepare for the great story of Holy Week and Easter by walking
> with Jesus on his path to the cross. Like millions of Christians
> across the world, and through the centuries, we are going to do
> this by following the Stations of the Cross. This is a simple way
> of hearing, reflecting and praying on the stations, the points on
> the path that led from Jesus' betrayal and arrest, through his trial
> and execution, to his burial. By doing this we will all be drawn in
> a new way into this story which defines our faith.
>
> We are going to do this though not by finding these stations
> in the landscape around us. Instead we will use this landscape to
> find things which help us reflect on these different parts of the
> story and so help tell this story for ourselves. There are seven
> stations in total. You will need to find five objects yourself and
> two objects which we have hidden for you to find.
>
> As with the traditional Stations of the Cross there is a short
> Bible verse for each station, something to think about, and a
> prayer. As you follow your own journey you might like to use
> these on your hunt. We will then use them all again when we
> gather back in God's Tent.

CREATING

The Stations of the Cross

1. Jesus prays at Gethsemane

Reading:

> They went to a place called Gethsemane; and he said to his disciples, "Sit here while I pray."
>
> *Mark 14:32*

Activity:

- Can you find somewhere really peaceful where you might pray and speak to God?
- Collect something from that place that reminds you of that place.

Prayer:

> Lord Jesus, you prepared for impending death by praying for strength from your Father. Help us to find the strength to find our strength in you. **Amen.**

2. Jesus is betrayed and arrested

Reading:

> Then Judas Iscariot, who was one of the twelve, went to the chief priests in order to betray him to them. When they heard it, they were greatly pleased, and promised to give him money . . . Judas, one of the twelve, arrived; and with him there was a crowd with swords and clubs, from the chief priests, the scribes, and the elders. Now the betrayer had given them a sign, saying, "The one

I will kiss is the man; arrest him and lead him away under guard."
So when he came, he went up to him at once and said, "Rabbi!"
and kissed him. Then they laid hands on him and arrested him.

Mark 14:10–11a, 43b–46

Activity:

- Judas was paid in silver by the chief priests to betray Jesus. Find
  where the payment has been left for you—is it finer than the other
  things you will collect today?
- Would this tempt you?

Prayer:

Lord Jesus, we all too easily find value in money and wealth.
Forgive us when we look for meaning and value in things other
than you. **Amen.**

3. Jesus is judged by Pilate

Reading:

Pilate asked them, "Why, what evil has he done?" But they
shouted all the more, "Crucify him!" So Pilate, wishing to satisfy
the crowd, released Barabbas for them; and after flogging Jesus,
he handed him over to be crucified.

Mark 15:14–15

Activity:

- Jesus was put on trial in front of Pilate, the Roman leader. He
  condemned Jesus to death, but first had him whipped and
  scourged. Can you use the string to make a scourge or whip by
  wrapping some sticks together?

Prayer:

> Lord Jesus, you were whipped and abused for no reason. Forgive us all for the ways in which we have harmed other people for no reason. **Amen.**

4. Jesus is crowned with a crown of thorns

Reading:

> And they clothed him in a purple cloak; and after twisting some thorns into a crown, they put it on him. And they began saluting him, "Hail, King of the Jews!"
>
> *Mark 15:17–18*

Activity:

- To make fun of Jesus his guards made him a crown of thorns not gold. Can you make a crown out of thorny branches?

Prayer:

> Lord Jesus, the guards laughed at you in the crown of thorns. Forgive us for making fun of other people. **Amen.**

5. Jesus carries his cross

Reading:

> After mocking him, they stripped him of the purple cloak and put his own clothes on him. Then they led him out to crucify him.
>
> *Mark 15:20*

Activity:

- Jesus said that we should take up our cross and follow him. Can you use the string to make a cross and carry it back to God's Tent?

Prayer:

Lord Jesus, you carried the weight of our sins as you carried the cross. Help us see the depth of your love for us. **Amen.**

6. Jesus is crucified

Reading:

Then they brought Jesus to the place called Golgotha (which means the place of a skull). And they offered him wine mixed with myrrh; but he did not take it. And they crucified him.

Mark 15:22-24a

Activity:

- The soldiers nailed Jesus to the cross to crucify him. Can you find something sharp like a nail?

Prayer:

Lord Jesus, you bled for us as you were nailed to the cross. Transform our suffering through the depths of your love. **Amen.**

7. Jesus is buried

Reading:

> When evening had come, and since it was the day of Preparation, that is, the day before the sabbath, Joseph of Arimathea, a respected member of the council, who was also himself waiting expectantly for the kingdom of God, went boldly to Pilate and asked for the body of Jesus . . . Then Joseph bought a linen cloth, and taking down the body, wrapped it in the linen cloth, and laid it in a tomb that had been hewn out of the rock. He then rolled a stone against the door of the tomb.
>
> *Mark 15:42–43,46*

Activity:

- How have you looked after a friend who is in need or who has suffered?
- Think about how Jesus' friends helped him even in death as you find and collect a piece of cloth.

Prayer:

> Lord Jesus, your friends laid you in the darkness of the tomb. Help us when we find ourselves in the dark places of life. **Amen.**

REFLECTING

With everyone gathered again in the tent, the worship continues by simply working through each of the stations one by one. As you do so invite different voices to read each of the Bible passages and use the questions above, or your own, to reflect on what this station tells us about the power of God's love revealed to us in the resurrection. As you work through the stations, ask people to show what they found and reflect on the questions that have been offered. As each conversation finishes, naturally gather it together with the short prayer and move to the next station.

DEPARTING

Once you have worked through each of the stations you might like to offer a simple extempory prayer, or you could use this prayer:

> Eternal God,
> in the cross of Jesus
> we see the cost of sin
> and the depth of your love:
> in humble hope and fear
> may we place at his feet
> all that we have and all that we are,
> through Jesus Christ our Lord.
> **Amen**
>
> *Church of England Alternative Collect for Good Friday*

The Lord's Prayer

Song suggestion: 'Were you there when they crucified my Lord?' (Traditional American spiritual)

Final Prayer:

> May God the Father walk with us as we leave his tent . . .

CHAPTER 9

Stations of the Resurrection
Scavenger Hunt

This pitching is designed for the weeks following Easter when we walk the Stations of the Resurrection and it works well in a pair with the previous pitching on the Stations of the Cross. The Stations of the Resurrection is the younger sibling to the older and more well-known Stations of the Cross. First developed in the Roman Catholic Church at the end of the last century, the Stations of the Resurrection encourage the faithful to mediate on the *via lucis*, the way of light, shown to us in Jesus' resurrection appearances.

The Stations of the Resurrection have become more well known in the Church of England following their inclusion in *Common Worship: Times and Seasons*.[39] In their traditional form, like the Stations of the Cross, there are fourteen Stations of the Resurrection. Seven have been chosen for this session. As with our interpretation of the Stations of the Cross, it might be that in running this yourself you choose a different selection, add more or subtract, depending on your need and context. As is so often the case with pitchings of God's Tent, it is the form, and not just the content, which is vital.

Where to pitch the tent

This pitching works best held in relation with the Stations of the Cross pitching. For this reason, you might want to consider the location for your pitching in relation to your pitching for the Stations of the Cross. One option would be to find somewhere lush and verdant in contrast to a wilder location for the Stations of the Cross. The other would be to gather in the same place. This has two benefits. The first is that it reminds us that the cross and resurrection are inseparable, that the place in which we look for the cross is also the place to look for signs of the resurrection. The second benefit, linked to this, is that there is a good chance you will be pitching these sessions either side of the boundary between winter and spring. So, you may be fortunate to return to a place which last month was barren but has now burst into new life—what better image of the resurrection could there be than that!

The most important thing is to find somewhere with lots of space to explore. The main activity is a scavenger hunt, and so you need things to scavenge. The pitching outlined below assumes that you will be near sheep, or at least pastureland. We also took the chance to hide one of the provided items (in this case, bread for the meal at Emmaus) as far from God's Tent as we could (about three-quarters of a mile away) to encourage everyone to explore as widely as possible. This had the benefit of providing space for conversation and reflection as we followed and searched for our Stations of the Resurrection.

What will you need (beyond the normal)

- Copies of the stations including the Bible readings. You might like to laminate them to make them waterproof and reusable.
- Small bags to collect things in.
- A piece of string per person.
- A basket of bread.
- A basket of strips of white cloth.

The Pitching

GATHERING

Song suggestion: Final verse of "Were you there when they crucified my Lord?" ("Were you there when he rose up from the tomb?")

Opening Prayer:

> When God led his people through the wilderness to the promised land . . .

Reading:

> And suddenly there was a great earthquake; for an angel of the Lord, descending from heaven, came and rolled back the stone and sat on it. His appearance was like lightning, and his clothing white as snow. For fear of him the guards shook and became like dead men.
>
> *Matthew 28:2–4*

Introduction: You might like to use this script or adapt the meaning into your own words.

> Happy Easter! We are now in those wonderful weeks after Easter when we come to understand what God has done for us all in the resurrection of Jesus Christ from the dead. This is not an easy idea to get hold of and if you struggle with it a little, don't worry; so did many of Jesus' closest friends. But rather than get annoyed with them for not seeing what had happened, Jesus appeared to them again and again, helping them to come to understand more deeply the new life and new possibilities that God puts in front of us in the resurrection.
>
> Today this is what we are going to do, by looking for signs or "stations" of the resurrection. There are seven in total. You

will need to scavenge for five, and two have been provided. Of the two we have provided, one is at the far end of the area we are exploring, and one is on the way there, so explore the whole space. As you scavenge for the remaining stations please only take things which are already on the ground—fallen leaves, branches, don't cut anything for this!

CREATING

The Stations of the Resurrection

1. The Empty Tomb (provided as a strip of white cloth hidden on the way)

Reading:

Early on the first day of the week, while it was still dark, Mary Magdalene came to the tomb and saw that the stone had been removed from the tomb. So she ran and went to Simon Peter and the other disciple, the one whom Jesus loved, and said to them, "They have taken the Lord out of the tomb, and we do not know where they have laid him." Then Peter and the other disciple set out and went towards the tomb. The two were running together, but the other disciple outran Peter and reached the tomb first. He bent down to look in and saw the linen wrappings lying there, but he did not go in. Then Simon Peter came, following him, and went into the tomb. He saw the linen wrappings lying there, and the cloth that had been on Jesus' head, not lying with the linen wrappings but rolled up in a place by itself. Then the other disciple, who reached the tomb first, also went in, and he saw and believed.

John 20:1–8

Activity:

- As you explore you will find a basket of linen cloths. Take one.
- What else could you use these cloths for? What might the link be to the resurrection and what God is telling through this?

Prayer:

Lord Jesus, before it was light your friends came to care for you at the tomb. Help us search for your light in the dark places of our world. **Amen.**

2. The Road to Emmaus (provided in bread hidden at the furthest extent of the space you are exploring)

Reading:

As they came near the village to which they were going, he walked ahead as if he were going on. But they urged him strongly, saying, "Stay with us, because it is almost evening and the day is now nearly over". So he went in to stay with them. When he was at the table with them, he took bread, blessed and broke it, and gave it to them. Then their eyes were opened, and they recognized him; and he vanished from their sight.

Luke 24:28–31

Activity:

- Make your way to the "roadside café" (you will need to explain where this is at the far extent of the space we are in) and find what is waiting for you. Collect what is there.
- Can you think of times you have shared a meal with a good friend? What was important about that meal?

Prayer:

> Risen Lord, you showed yourself to your friends in the breaking
> of bread. Help us find you present when we share your truth with
> others. **Amen.**

3. Jesus shares his Peace

Reading:

> When it was evening on that day, the first day of the week, and
> the doors of the house where the disciples had met were locked
> for fear of the Jews, Jesus came and stood among them and said,
> "Peace be with you." After he said this, he showed them his hands
> and his side. Then the disciples rejoiced when they saw the Lord.
> Jesus said to them again, "Peace be with you."
>
> *John 20:19–21a*

Activity:

- Find something that represents "peace" for you.
- I wonder what we can do to share the peace Jesus shares with us.
- Why is it important to do this?

Prayer:

> Lord Jesus, you bring peace to a broken world. Help us be signs
> and symbols of that peace. **Amen.**

4. Jesus breathes his Spirit on the disciples

Reading:

> Jesus said to them again, "Peace be with you. As the Father has sent me, so I send you." When he had said this, he breathed on them and said to them, "Receive the Holy Spirit. If you forgive the sins of any, they are forgiven them; if you retain the sins of any, they are retained."
>
> *John 20:21–23*

Activity:

- Using your string, can you make something that helps us see the wind of the Spirit all around us?
- How does this help you think about God's Spirit being with us all?

Prayer:

> Risen God, you give us the gift of your Spirit. May the Spirit guide us as we serve you in your world. **Amen.**

5. Jesus appears to "Doubting Thomas"

Reading:

> A week later his disciples were again in the house, and Thomas was with them. Although the doors were shut, Jesus came and stood among them and said, "Peace be with you." Then he said to Thomas, "Put your finger here and see my hands. Reach out your hand and put it in my side. Do not doubt but believe." Thomas answered him, "My Lord and my God!"
>
> *John 20:26–28*

Activity:

- Can you collect something sharp that might have made those marks in Jesus' body?
- I wonder why it was important for the resurrected Jesus to show his wounds?

Prayer:

Lord Jesus, when we doubt you, do not doubt our desire to love and serve you as our King and our God. **Amen.**

6. Feed my lambs

Reading:

When they had finished breakfast, Jesus said to Simon Peter, "Simon son of John, do you love me more than these?" He said to him, "Yes, Lord; you know that I love you." Jesus said to him, "Feed my lambs."

John 21:15

Activity:

- Hopefully you will be able to hear and see lambs in the fields nearby.
- Being sensible, can you collect something that reminds you of what it means to "feed my lambs"? What does it mean when Jesus asks us to "feed my lambs"?

Prayer:

Jesus our shepherd, tend us with your love so that we might tend your world. **Amen.**

7. Jesus commissions the disciples on the mountain

Reading:

> Now the eleven disciples went to Galilee, to the mountain to
> which Jesus had directed them. When they saw him, they
> worshipped him; but some doubted. And Jesus came and said to
> them, "All authority in heaven and on earth has been given to me.
> Go therefore and make disciples of all nations, baptizing them
> in the name of the Father and of the Son and of the Holy Spirit,
> and teaching them to obey everything that I have commanded
> you. And remember, I am with you always, to the end of the age."
>
> *Matthew 28:16–20*

Activity:

- Can you find the highest point where we are?
- When you get there, collect something to tell us where that was.
- Why was it important for Jesus to "commission" us from a high place?
- How important does that make this commission to us?

Prayer:

> Ascended God, as you join earth to heaven, may we bring your
> heavenly kingdom into a broken world. **Amen.**

REFLECTING

With everyone gathered again in the tent the worship continues by simply
working through each of the stations one by one. As you do so invite
different voices to read each of the Bible passages and use the questions
above, or your own, to reflect on what this station tells us about the power
of God's love revealed to us in the resurrection. As you work through the
stations, ask people to show what they found and reflect on the questions

that have been offered. If you have managed to pitch in the same location that you used for the Stations of the Cross, you might find it fruitful to compare the experience of searching for the Stations of the Cross and Resurrection in the same place. What does that tell us about the relationship between the cross and resurrection?

DEPARTING

Prayer: Once you have worked through each of the stations you might like to offer a simple extemporary prayer, or you could use this prayer:

> Risen Christ,
> for whom no door is locked, no entrance barred:
> open the doors of our hearts,
> that we may seek the good of others
> and walk the joyful road of sacrifice and peace,
> to the praise of God the Father.
> **Amen**
>
> *Church of England Alternative Collect*
> *for the second Sunday of Easter*

The Lord's Prayer

Song suggestion: "Surrexit Christus" in *Christ is risen, sing to the Lord* (Taizé Community, 1984).

Final Prayer:

> May God the Father walk with us as we leave his tent . . .

CHAPTER 10

Wise and Foolish Builders—Den Building

At the heart of the Gospels are Jesus' parables: short, memorable and beguiling stories which reveal to us something of who God is for us in Jesus, and what a life built on faith might look like. The stories run deep into our collective conscience. Just think about how many of these stories find their way into our everyday language. We speak of "good Samaritans", "prodigal sons" and of building on "rock or sand" without always remembering the full details of the parables from which they come. The more we read these parables, the more we discover that they are complex and challenging stories which we can study over and over again. They are, in the words of Cranmer's famous collect, those parts of the Bible we want to "read, mark, learn, and inwardly digest".[40]

There are many ways to do this, but one of the most powerful is the Benedictine pattern of *lectio divina* or divine reading. In *lectio divina* we are not so much reading the text, as allowing it to be digested and assimilated by a process of prayerful contemplation. In the classic formulation in Benedictine spirituality this is by the four-fold form of reading, meditation, prayer and contemplation. Absorbing the words of scripture into ourselves through this deep and prayerful reading, we are able to focus less on what this passage means, and more on what God is asking of us in these words. This might be through the prompt of a specific phrase that we reflect on, or even a single word. Through contemplation we are then drawn not to simply understand what God is saying to us in scripture, but to change our behaviour and act on this.

In our pitchings of God's Tent, we have found that the deep pattern of *lectio divina* has provided a powerful model to help us reflect on what God is saying to us in scripture, and particularly through the parables of Jesus. Although this pitching does not follow the strict pattern of *lectio divina* it does follow the spirit. By reflecting on these parables in the landscape we are able to use the glory of creation as the partner in our contemplation. By living out the deep meaning of this parable we are able to hear the words speak more clearly to us than when they are simply read or heard. Using the simple activity of den building, we are able to not only think about, but also to know, what it means to live out a life that is built on rock and not on sand.

Where to pitch the tent

Den building, as any eight-year-old will tell you, is always best done in the woods. Even in quite built-up areas you can find small pockets of woodland in which to build dens. If you can find a place with open space nearby to pitch God's Tent, that is even better. This might be in woods on the edge of or in a park, by some farmland, or even in the grounds of the church. The main thing, as always, is to have the cooperation and agreement of the landowner not only to pitch the tent, but also to build dens in the woods.

What will you need (beyond the normal)

- Nothing. Den building is best done with what you find there. Using string, plastic and foreign objects is, essentially, cheating!

What you might need to think of to keep everyone safe (beyond the normal)

- Be clear about the space you are using. Woods can be deceptive, especially with overgrowth. Be clear about the locations where you are going to work. If possible, work in mixed groups, ensuring there is an adult in each group.
- Make it clear that we are to use only what we can find on the floor already. That means there is no need to pull down, break or cut

any branches or overgrowth. You need to be able, if needed, to return the site to how you found it when you finish.

The Pitching

GATHERING

Song suggestion: "Heaven and Earth" in John L. Bell, *Come all you People: Shorter songs for worship* (Glasgow: Wild Goose Publications, 1994).

Opening Prayer:

> When God led his people through the wilderness to the promised land . . .

Welcome: You might want to use this following script:

> Jesus was an amazing teacher. Thousands of people would gather to hear him speak, and in hearing him their lives would be changed. One of the ways in which he taught was through stories or parables. These parables were special for two reasons. The first is that they were memorable. You could hear them and remember them and perhaps even repeat them to a friend. The second was that in these stories Jesus did not always give us the answer in a simple way but told the story to help us work out the answer for ourselves.
>
> Today we are going to hear one of those parables and use it to make sense of what God is saying to us in it.

Reading:

Jesus said: "Everyone then who hears these words of mine and acts on them will be like a wise man who built his house on rock. The rain fell, the floods came, and the winds blew and beat on that house, but it did not fall, because it had been founded on rock. And everyone who hears these words of mine and does not act on them will be like a foolish man who built his house on sand. The rain fell, and the floods came, and the winds blew and beat against that house, and it fell—and great was its fall!"

Matthew 7:24–27

Now, we could spend lots of time trying to understand what it means to be a wise builder or a foolish builder. But it would be better just to be a builder. So, we are going to go into the woods and build dens together, look and admire how splendid our dens are, and then come back and think whether we have been wise or foolish builders.

CREATING

Divide into groups and go off to make dens in the woods. Give everyone a rough time limit, say thirty to forty minutes. There are no restrictions or instructions on what to do or how to do it, but to make the best den you can. It works well if one person moves between the groups to see how things are progressing.

When everyone is finished or the time is up, gather everyone together and have a look at the different dens. Talk about what you like in each other's dens, what makes them similar and what makes them different. Once this is done return to God's Tent.

REFLECTING

When everyone is gathered in God's Tent read the passage again. Then after some silence ask:

> So, what made your den a good den; what made you a wise builder?

From running this session, we have had varied responses to this question, but it has usually included: choosing the ground well; having a good structure; working as a team; making it hospitable. Let this conversation flow and don't worry if it goes off in different directions. The key is to reflect on what you have done and what you have enjoyed doing.

When this part of the conversation has come to a natural end read the passage again—perhaps this time with a different reader. Then after some silence say:

> In this passage Jesus asks us to hear his words and act on them. In another translation of this passage he says that his words are "words to build a life on". So, if we were to build our lives in the way we built our dens as wise builders, what would that mean?

Hopefully people will draw from the observations they used before, such as being built on good foundations, on being well structured, on being hospitable. If they don't, you might like to use a leading question drawing on one of these examples like:

> One of you said your den was good because . . . how would your life be good if you built it that way?

When this conversation draws to a close, read the passage again, using a different reader again if possible.

DEPARTING

In this context the prayers work best off-the-cuff, building on the examples and ideas you have explored together, giving thanks for each of the themes in turn, and committing to live in this way going forward. You might like to gather this time of prayer together with this, or a similar, prayer.

> Father God, you invite each of us to build our lives on the words of your Son, Jesus Christ. Forgive us for those times when we have been foolish and not built on the rock of your word. Through your Spirit give us patience to build our lives on the sure foundations of your love. **Amen.**

The Lord's Prayer

Song suggestion: "For yours is the kingdom" in John L. Bell, *Come all you People: Shorter songs for worship* (Glasgow: Wild Goose Publications, 1994).

Final Prayer:

> May God the Father walk with us as we leave his tent . . .

CHAPTER 11

God's Tent Baptism

From earliest times churches have been defined not by how they are led, or by the kind of building they meet in, or the parts of scripture they use. The thing that has defined churches as communities following the truth revealed by God in Jesus Christ is that, in their actions, they follow two of Jesus' central commands. The first is that they share bread and wine "in remembrance of me" (1 Corinthians 11:24). The second is that, following the great commission at the end of Matthew's Gospel, these communities make disciples and baptize "in the name of the Father and of the Son, and of the Holy Spirit" (Matthew 28:19). Churches do many things, but the one thing a church should always do is make disciples of Jesus Christ, and help these disciples to confirm this commitment in the sacrament of Holy Baptism. As a new expression of Church, God's Tent draws on this ancient heritage and has become a place where disciples have been made. It is therefore fitting that these disciples have come to their public affirmation of faith not in a "proper" church, but in this new church, a baptized and baptizing community, pitched among us.

This pitching describes how all those gathered to God's Tent might engage in and come to understand the symbols of baptism. In this way this pitching could work both as a stand-alone session focusing on the reaffirmation of baptism vows or, as we have used it, as part of a baptism service itself for adults and young people able to make the promises of baptism on their own behalf. Outlined below is, therefore, only part of what might be used in a God's Tent baptism as the baptism liturgy itself has been left for you to form in a way which is fitting for your tradition and denomination. What is the same for all of us, and what is the focus of this pitching, are the symbols and signs that define baptism: the anointing with oil, the baptism in water and the giving of a lighted candle. Each of these is explored in the form of a prayer station with which those gathered to this pitching can engage in their own time and own way. Candidates for baptism can then use this as a means of understanding more personally the symbols that are part of their baptism. Others can use this to reflect on the enduring power of these symbols, conferred on them at their baptism, and what they mean to their ongoing journey of faith.

The great opportunity in this pitching is to show the enormity of God's love revealed to us in baptism. A traditional church baptism is a beautiful occasion, but often we are a little sparing, even apologetic, with the symbols. We anoint with the smallest smear of oil, baptize with a shell full of water, give the light of Christ in a small candle. In this exploration of baptism, in the vastness of creation we can have symbols which expand into the space God's made for us all in the overflowing gift of his love. So, the anointing can be with a jug of oil running down the anointed "like the precious oil on the head . . . of Aaron, running down over the collar of his robes" (Psalm 133:2). The water of baptism, whether by full submersion or just a good dunking, can be like the "flowing streams" which the deer longs for, that mirror our longing for God (Psalm 42:1). The light can be given from a great fire reminding us that "God is light and in him there is no darkness at all" (1 John 1:5b).

Where to pitch the tent

Whether this pitching includes a baptism or is a reflection on baptism, it is best done by a river or the sea. Around it you will also need to make space to set up the prayer stations so that those gathered can spend time at each station without feeling rushed or cramped.

What will you need (beyond the normal)

- Prayer stations—the details of which are listed below.
- If this is a baptism, you will also need to prepare a suitable baptism liturgy (we used a version of the Church of England liturgy).

What you might need to think of to keep everyone safe (beyond the normal)

There are always dangers in being based near open water. If you are going to go into the water for the baptism, ensure that you know where the safe points for entry are, and that those joining you for the baptism are suitably prepared.

The Pitching

GATHERING

Song suggestion: "Come Holy Spirit, descend on us" in John L. Bell, *Come all you People: Shorter songs for worship* (Glasgow: Wild Goose Publications, 1994).

Opening Prayer:

> When God led his people through the wilderness to the promised land . . .

Reading:

> Now the eleven disciples went to Galilee, to the mountain to which Jesus had directed them. When they saw him, they worshipped him; but some doubted. And Jesus came and said to them, "All authority in heaven and on earth has been given to me. Go therefore and make disciples of all nations, baptizing them in the name of the Father and of the Son and of the Holy Spirit, and teaching them to obey everything that I have commanded you. And remember, I am with you always, to the end of the age."
> *Matthew 28:16–20*

Welcome: You might like to use this script or similar words of instruction:

Before the Church had buildings, or vicars, or bishops, the Church did two things. The first was to share bread and wine as Jesus commanded us to "in remembrance of me". The second was that they followed Jesus' "great commission", which we have just heard, to baptize disciples. And that is what we have come to do today. But at the heart of any baptism service is not just the promises that these candidates are about to make. It is a chance for each one of us to reconnect with the signs and symbols of our baptism, and through that to recommit ourselves to our own faith in Jesus.

At the heart of the service of baptism are three symbols, three signs which point us to what God is doing for all who come to him in faith. The first is oil for anointing, showing we are marked out for and by God as special in God's sight. The second is water, which refreshes and cleans us. The third is light, to remind us of Jesus, the light of the world, who the darkness can never overcome.

Set out around us are three prayer stations for each of us to spend some time with, to reflect on these symbols of baptism and, as we come to the service of baptism, to know again what they will mean for these candidates and for us, as we all commit ourselves in faith to our God who is pitched among us.

CREATING

Prayer Stations

1. Oil

What you need:

- A large sealed jar of oil and balsamic vinegar, the larger the better.
- The Bible reading, activity and prayer, available for each person to read.

Reading: (available for those coming to the station to read)

> You prepare a table before me in the presence of my enemies;
> you anoint my head with oil; my cup overflows.
>
> *Psalm 23:5-6*

Activity:

- Shake the jar (I know it's salad dressing but bear with me!)
- Can you stop the oil being mixed with the darkness?
- What happens as oil separates from the darkness?
- What does it mean to be anointed—to be sanctified, marked out—for God with oil?

Prayer:

> God of light and love, you call each of us by name. Help me to remember that as I am anointed, I am precious in your sight.
> **Amen.**

2. Water

What you need:

- A place near the water where you can get your hands or feet really muddy and dirty.
- The Bible reading, activity and prayer, available for each person to read.

Reading:

"Those who drink of the water that I will give them will never be thirsty. The water that I will give will become in them a spring of water gushing up to eternal life."

John 4:14

Activity:

- Get down into the water, get wet, get your hands dirty in the mud, run your hands through the water. What happens?
- What do we wash away with water every day without thinking?
- What does God wash away for us in his love each day?

Prayer:

Living God, in the waters of baptism you wash away our faults and fears. Help us to live refreshed and renewed by your saving love. **Amen.**

3. Light

What you need:

- Some form of constant flame. This could be a steady fire or an oil lamp.
- The Bible reading, activity and prayer, available for each person to read.

Reading:

> "You are the light of the world. A city built on a hill cannot be hidden. No one after lighting a lamp puts it under the bushel basket, but on the lampstand, and it gives light to all in the house. In the same way, let your light shine before others, so that they may see your good works and give glory to your Father in heaven."
>
> *Matthew 5:14–16*

Activity:

- What would happen if we covered this light?
- What can we do with this light when it is not hidden?
- What does it feel like to be called "the light of the world"?

Prayer:

> God of Light, in Jesus you give us the light of the world. Help us shine that light into the dark places of our lives and the world in your name. **Amen.**

REFLECTING

Once everyone has spent time with the prayer stations, you will gather again in God's Tent. What happens next depends on whether this will be part of a formal baptism, or simply a reflection on baptism. Either way it is good to spend some time reflecting on each of the symbols and what those gathered understood in them. It might be that you use the prayers again to sum up each discussion.

If you move into a baptism, as you come to each of the symbols you might like to pause on them and give everyone the chance to reflect on that symbol, using the prayer to draw their experience of the prayer stations and their use in the baptism service together. You might even like to retain the prayer stations, moving around them as you move through the baptism liturgy.

The following prayers and blessing can be used as part of this pitching, whether in a service of baptism or a reflection on baptism.

DEPARTING

Prayer:

> Almighty Father,
> you have made us heirs through hope of
>   your everlasting kingdom,
> and in the waters of baptism you have promised
> a measure of grace overflowing to all eternity.
> Take our sins and guilt away,
> and so inflame us with the life of your Spirit
> that we may know your favour and goodness towards us,
> and walk in newness of life, both now and for ever;
> through Jesus Christ your Son our Lord,
> who is alive and reigns with you,
> in the unity of the Holy Spirit,
> one God, now and for ever. **Amen.**[41]

The Lord's Prayer

Final Prayer:

> May God the Father walk with us as we leave his tent . . .

Conclusion

The picture of a tent-pitching God is as old as time. However, God's Tent, as a reflection of that image, is still in its infancy. This book has tried to reflect on the ageless power of this metaphor within the challenges and opportunities being faced by the contemporary Church. It is not a perfect expression of church; what is? But it is an attempt to draw afresh on the ancient wisdom of the Church and our faith as we find a new way to respond to God's call within creation. Even if God's Tent is in its infancy, some of its character is beginning to emerge. This conclusion is an attempt to capture some of what this emerging character is by asking: "What is God's Tent?"

God's Tent is . . . about Jesus

This first observation would seem self-evident, not simply for God's Tent but also for all expressions of church however old they might be. However, this is an observation which is worth making again: God's Tent has Jesus at the centre. We can, as the Church, be a little reticent about talking about Jesus and communicating to the world who he was and is for us. Something of this comes from a fear that the language of "Jesus" will put people off, and so we speak in a more measured way of "God" or "the Church" instead. But Jesus Christ is the foundation of our faith. Jesus is, as Paul reminds the church in Ephesus, "the breadth and length and height and depth" of our faith (Ephesians 3:18). For this reason, it is essential that as we go out to meet people—those whom the *Mission-shaped Church* report described as the de-churched and non-churched—we come to them with a powerful picture of who Jesus is: not simply a good man who lived some time ago, or an idea to lead us to God, but God's whole-self revealed in Jesus Christ, pitched among us.

In this way, God's Tent is incarnational. It reflects again and again on the idea of a God who comes down the mountain, who takes our flesh and lives among us and with us. As we live in a society which increasingly does not look for meaning within the shelter of a church building, God's Tent allows us to take that fixed sense of God's presence out to where people already are. As we have seen in the sample pitchings outlined in this book, not all the pitchings revolve around a story of Jesus. But by locating these stories in God's Tent we are reinforcing that, through our faith, all these stories lead us to the same truth, that Jesus Christ is Lord.

God's Tent is . . . immediate and elusive

To say that God's Tent is incarnational is not to say that it is either domesticated or over-familiar. As we read through the story of the Exodus, it is clear that the God we meet in the Tent is still a mysterious and elusive God. Even in the tent of the wilderness, in the immediacy of God speaking to Moses "face to face, as one speaks to a friend", this was still a mysterious and elusive presence, shrouded in the pillar of cloud (Exodus 33:7–11). As we encounter God, pitched among us in Jesus, in the Gospels Jesus is always both an immediate and yet elusive figure. When Mary Magdalene, overcome with the joy of Easter morning, flings her arms around Jesus he says cryptically, "Do not hold on to me, because I have not yet ascended to my Father" (John 20:17). To know God is to know this immediate and elusive presence. It is that sense of God which R. S. Thomas so famously describes in his poem *The Absence* as that presence which has just left a room one enters;[42] or, in Ann Lewin's beautiful image of prayer, like waiting for a kingfisher by simply being where it is likely to appear, based only on the knowledge that it has been there.[43] To know God is to seek always the elusive nature of that immediacy, moving ahead of us, waiting for us to catch up.

We have found that God's Tent is a place which is both immediate and elusive. It is immediate in its relative informality, in the comfort and warmth, which are described in chapter 4, that we seek to create there. It is immediate in the relationships and conversations that it encourages and creates, and in that there is an immediacy to the experience of faith

that it creates. But this is still elusive. The impermanence of God's Tent—
we arrive, pitch, worship and leave within three hours—means that it is
not a fixed place. It is a place where we can glimpse something of the
God who moves among us and in front of us; the God who was there
before we arrived, who calls us into relationship and moves ahead of us,
calling us to follow.

God's Tent is . . . small

God's Tent began life in a deeply rural context. That is not to say that it
is an idea that can only exist within this context, but it will always have
something of that DNA running through it wherever it may find itself.
At the heart of the DNA of the rural church is the reality that it is a small
church. The average weekly attendance in a rural church is thirty-six. In
an urban parish it is ninety-nine. That is not to say that rural churches are
shrinking. In fact the number of churches that are growing numerically
in the rural church is the same as in the urban church, around 18 per
cent.[44] But the reality is that in cardinal figures those rural churches will,
in the main, be beginning from a lower numerical base than their urban
counterparts. It is important to state this reality because we live in a
church which, because of the explicit focus on growing the church, has
by default come to focus on and celebrate the large. There is nothing
intrinsically wrong with this, but it must always be held in creative
tension with the value of the small. So, as we mark the flourishing of
the large, we should not be afraid also to celebrate and rejoice in the
faithfulness of the small.

This is a central insight of our faith. Through all of scripture God again
and again looks to the small to bring about transformation and hope in
the world. Through Genesis we hear again and again that the younger
son—Isaac not Ishmael, Jacob not Esau, Joseph not the elder brothers—is
the means through which God's transforming promise is known. In the
promised land God does not choose one of the economic or military
powerhouses of the ancient world; he chooses a small but flourishing
land, flowing in "milk and honey", for his chosen people. In the prophetic
voices of the Old Testament we find again and again that it is the small

which is crucial: the birds that feed Elijah (1 Kings 17), the little girl who led Naaman to Elisha (2 Kings 5); and it is through the "still small voice of calm" that God reveals himself to Elijah (1 Kings 19). This theme of the small continues into the New Testament and into what Rowan Williams described as "God's small initiative", where a tiny baby, born in a small town on the edge of empire, has the destiny to change the world.[45]

All of this reminds us, particularly in a time when we focus so much on the large, that God also works in and through the small. God's Tent is, by definition, small. In our pitching we are limited by those who will make the additional effort to find where we are. When we gather, we are limited by those who can fit into the tent. Our pattern of worship and exploration assumes that small groups will act and reflect and work together. None of this is to claim a moral superiority for the small over the large. In scripture we find pictures of the abundance and overflowing largeness of God's grace—the wedding at Cana and the feeding of the five thousand, for instance. We find this wonder in God's abundance every time we pitch God's Tent in the beauty of our landscape and creation, and what could be a more eloquent expression of God's grandeur than that? But God's Tent, in and of itself, is small, and we rejoice in that. If it were large, well, firstly we'd need a bigger tent, and secondly it would lose something of that DNA, that God reveals to us in the small.

God's Tent is . . . fragile

As many who work in the rural church and other "small" contexts know all too well, the cost of small is that it is also fragile. One or two people can literally make the difference between a church that feels it is flourishing and one which is floundering. This is an experience we have come to know all too well in our pitchings of God's Tent. There have been occasions where the small group of leaders has gathered, pitched the tent and waited, often more in hope than expectation that people will come. I am not afraid to say that there have been times when this has led me to feel a little downhearted, a little anxious that in our smallness there is a fragility from which we could not begin to flourish. However, like the recognition of smallness, it is also important to remember that God's grace works through fragility. John Thomson—Bishop of Selby and the Archbishop of York's ambassador on Rural Life and Faith—reminds us that fragility runs through the stories of God's life with his people. As Thomson argues:

> The Church proclaims a Gospel whose central figure is the kenotic Christ, God incarnate whose mission strategy involved self-emptying and working with a dysfunctional group of disciples in ways which exposed them as signs of his Kingdom to the judgement of their peers.[46]

Fragility is not just a reality of faith; it is the pattern and mode of the missional life which God calls us to join.

In this way the implicit fragility of God's Tent is not something to be anxious about, but something which is intrinsic to its very identity. God's Tent is fragile, literally. When the wind blows and the rain falls—as it has been known to do once or twice in Northumberland—sometimes it is only the fragile width of the tent's canvas that shelters us from the wilds of the world around us. To worship in God's Tent is to be in a fragile place. It can be uncomfortable (not everyone likes sitting on the ground) and it can be cold and wet and muddy. To worship God is to be in a fragile place, as we open our true selves to God. But in these places that make us fragile we must remember that God does not call us to be comfortable. God calls us to follow his Son, who made himself fragile for our sake.

God's Tent . . . shows us his glory

In chapter 3 we remembered the popular trope of the Christmas sermon which, drawing on John 1:14, reminds us that "the Word became flesh and *pitched his tent (skénoó)* among us". In many ways this book, and for that matter the whole of the God's Tent project, is a reflection on the richness of this one verse. There is, however, a danger not only in the well-meaning Christmas sermon but also in God's Tent itself that we get so caught up in the vividness of this picture that we fail to read the whole verse. If we stop with the tent, literally and figuratively, we are in danger of missing the deeper truth to which the carefully chosen language of this verse is pointing us.

As we have already seen, there is an etymological line that draws us towards our tent-pitching God, not only in the prologue to John's Gospel, but also in the stories of David and back to the story of the Exodus. In grasping at this etymological thread there is a danger that we miss the full wealth of what the original hearers of John's Gospel would have heard. The language of the original Greek would have drawn its first hearers not only from *skénoó* to the picture of a tent (*skéné*), but also to the Hebrew, *shekhinah*, or glory of God. To recognize the presence of a tent-pitching God was to recognize this tent as the beginning and not the end of that encounter with God. In the Tent of Meeting of the Exodus, God's glory, *shekhinah*, was revealed. So, in John's Prologue it is not enough to say that God, in Jesus, has pitched his tent among us. Rather this decisive act of divine tent-pitching leads us to see in Jesus the truth we discover when we read all of John 1:14 that, "the Word became flesh and lived among us, and we have seen his glory, the glory as of a father's only son, full of grace and truth".

To discover God revealed in his tent is not the end of our journey; it is only the beginning. In this way God's Tent is not, and can never be, an end in itself. God's Tent is a means of glimpsing God's glory, and in the experience beginning a journey to discover more. That is why we work so hard to navigate the frontier between the inheritance of the Church and the innovation it is called to discover. That is why we work to "tether" our expression of God's Tent to the other patterns and expressions of church within our parishes. It is also why we use different patterns and traditions of spirituality within our pitchings. Through all of these we want to encourage those drawn to God's Tent, whether they are from the heart or fringe of church life, whether they are de-churched or non-churched, to look for more; to continue to seek a relationship with the living God, whose glory is revealed when he pitches his tent among us.

Notes

1   Walter Brueggemann, *An Introduction to the Old Testament: The Canon and Christian Imagination* (Louisville, KY and London: Westminster John Knox Press, 2003), pp. 1–13.

2   N. T. Wright, *The New Testament and the People of God* (London: SPCK, 1992), pp. 139–44; Bruce Ellis Benson, "Improvising Texts, Improvising Communities: Jazz, Interpretation, Heterophony, and the *Ekklēsia*", in Jeremy S. Begbie and Steven R. Guthrie (eds), *Resonant Witness: Conversations between Music and Theology* (Grand Rapids, MI and Cambridge, UK: William Eerdmans Publishing Company, 2011), pp. 295–319.

3   Rory Stewart, *The Marches: Border Walks with My Father* (London: Jonathan Cape, 2016), p. 28.

4   John Milbank, "Stale Expressions: The Management Shaped Church", *Studies in Christian Ethics* 21 (2008), pp. 117–28, here at p. 124.

5   Pete Ward, *Liquid Church* (Carlisle: Paternoster Press, 2002), p. 1.

6   Stephen B. Bevans and Roger P. Schroeder, *Constants in Context: A Theology of Mission for Today* (Maryknoll, NY: Orbis Books, 2004), p. 1.

7   Christopher J. H. Wright, *The Mission of God: Unlocking the Bible's Grand Narrative* (Nottingham: InterVarsity Press, 2006), p. 46.

8   For an overview of this sociological change, see Linda Woodhead, "Introduction", in Linda Woodhead and Rebecca Catto (eds), *Religion and Change in Modern Britain* (London and New York: Routledge, 2012), pp. 1–33.

9   *Mission-shaped Church: Church Planting and Fresh Expressions of Church in a Changing World* (London: Church House Publishing, 2004), p. 9.

10 Andrew Davison and Alison Milbank, *For the Parish: A Critique of Fresh Expressions* (London: SCM Press, 2010), p. 102.

11 Davison and Milbank, *For the Parish*, p. 22.

12 Ibid., p. 163.

13 Ibid., p. 41.

[14]   "A programme for reform and renewal GS 1976", <hhttps://www. churchofengland.org/about/renewal-reform>, accessed on 4 July 2019.

[15]   Ibid.

[16]   All figures taken from, or extrapolated from, "Released for mission, growing the rural church GS Misc 1092", <https//www.churchofengland.org/more/ media-centre/news/released-mission-growing-rural-church>, accessed 4 July 2019.

[17]   See *A new measure of poverty for the UK* (London: Social Metrics Commission, 2018).

[18]   Figures taken from "Summary of projects funded" found at <https://www. churchofengland.org/more/diocesan-resources/funding-mission-and- growth/strategic-development-funding>, accessed on 4 July 2019.

[19]   Rowan Williams, "Theological resources for re-examining Church", in Steven Croft (ed.), *The Future of the Parish System: Shaping the Church of England for the 21st Century* (London: Church House Publishing, 2006), pp. 49–60, and here at pp. 54–55.

[20]   Ibid., p. 53.

[21]   Rowan Williams, "What is Catholic Orthodoxy?", in Kenneth Leech and Rowan Williams (eds), *Essays Catholic and Radical* (London: Bowerdean Press, 1983), pp. 14–19, and here at p. 18.

[22]   Simon Oliver, "The Cathedral and Rooted Growth", in Stephen Platten (ed.), *Holy Ground: Cathedrals in the twenty-first century* (Durham: Sacristy Press, 2017), pp. 23–40, and here at p. 25.

[23]   Oliver, "The Cathedral and Rooted Growth", p. 25.

[24]   Bevans and Schroeder, *Constants in Context*, pp. 21–22.

[25]   Bruce Stanley, *Forest Church: A Field Guide to Nature Connection for Groups and Individuals* (Llangurig: Mystic Christ Press, 2013), p. 12.

[26]   Quoted at <https://www.godforall.org.uk/mountain-pilgrims>, accessed on 4 July 2019.

[27]   Terence E. Fretheim, *Exodus: Interpretation, a Bible Commentary for Teaching and Preaching* (Louisville, KY: John Knox Press, 1991), pp. 272–76.

[28]   Michael Sadgrove, *Landscapes of Faith: The Christian Heritage of the North-East* (London: Third Millennium Publishing, 2013), pp. 90–91.

[29]   Benjamin Carter, "'A Serious House on Serious Earth': Toward an Understanding of the Church of England's Inheritance of Buildings", *Journal of Anglican Studies*, 16(2) (2018), pp. 128–46.

30 Sally Gaze, *Mission-shaped and Rural: Growing Churches in the Countryside* (London: Church House Publishing, 2006), p. 95.

31 Richard Giles, *Repitching the Tent: The Definitive Guide to Re-ordering Church Buildings for Worship and Mission*, 3rd edn. (Norwich: Canterbury Press, 2004), p. 15.

32 Walter Brueggemann, *First and Second Samuel: Interpretation, A Commentary for Teaching and Preaching* (Louisville, KT: John Knox, 1990), p. 253.

33 Brueggemann, *First and Second Samuel*, p. 254.

34 Giles, *Repitching the Tent*, p. 25.

35 Brueggemann, *An Introduction to the Old Testament*, p. 63.

36 <https://www.uknea.unep-wcmc.org/>, accessed on 4 July 2019; "The great myth of urban Britain", <https://www.bbc.co.uk/news/uk-18623096>, accessed on 4 July 2019.

37 David Atkinson, *Renewing the Face of the Earth: A Theological and Pastoral Response to Climate Change* (Norwich: Canterbury Press, 2008), p. 41.

38 Peter Pesic, *Music and the Making of Modern Science* (Boston, MA: MIT Press, 2014), pp. 121–32.

39 *Common Worship: Times and Seasons* (London: Church House Publishing, 2006), pp. 443–68.

40 Collect for the second Sunday in Advent, in *The Book of Common Prayer*.

41 Collect of Baptism from All Saints' Day until Advent, in *Common Worship: Christian Initiation* (London: Church House Publishing, 2005).

42 R. S. Thomas, *Selected Poems* (London: Penguin Books, 2004), p. 133.

43 Ann Lewin, "Disclosure", in *Watching for the Kingfisher: Poems and Prayers* (Norwich: Canterbury Press, 2009), p. 31.

44 "Released for mission, growing the rural church", pp. 9–10.

45 <http://aoc2013.brix.fatbeehive.com/articles.php/2755/archbishops-bbc-radio-2-pause-for-thought-message-christmas-is-gods-small-initiative>.

46 John B. Thomson, "Friendship in Fragility: A Gospel for the North?", in Gavin Wakefield and Nigel Rooms (eds), *Northern Gospel, Northern Church: Reflection on Identity and Mission* (Durham: Sacristy Press, 2016), pp. 93–104, and here at p. 95.

Lightning Source UK Ltd.
Milton Keynes UK
UKHW020756270322
400663UK00005B/475